THE TIME
BETWEEN

Cycles and Rhythms
in Ordinary Time

Wendy M. Wright

UPPER
ROOM BOOKS™

The Time Between
© 1999 Wendy M. Wright.
All rights reserved.

No part of this book may be reproduced in any manner whatsoever without written permission of the publisher except in brief quotations embodied in critical articles or reviews.
For information address The Upper Room®, 1908 Grand Avenue, Nashville, Tennessee
37212.

Upper Room® Web address: http://www.upperroom.org

UPPER ROOM®, UPPER ROOM BOOKS™ and design logos are trademarks owned by
the Upper Room®, Nashville, Tennessee. All rights reserved.

All scripture quotations unless otherwise noted are from The New Revised Standard Version of the Bible, copyright © 1989 by the Division of Christian Education of the National
Council of the Churches of Christ in the United States of America. Used by permission.

Scripture texts designated NEB are from The New English Bible. © The Delegates of Oxford University Press and The Syndics of the Cambridge University Press 1961, 1970.
Reprinted with permission.

Scripture texts designated REB are from The Revised English Bible (a revision of The New
English Bible) and © Oxford University Press and Cambridge University Press 1989.
Reprinted with permission.

Pages 238–239 constitute an extension of the copyright page.

Cover Design: Leigh Ann Dans
Cover Illustration: *Water Lilies* by Monet. Christie's Images/Superstock
Interior Design: Charles Sutherland
First Printing: 1999

The Library of Congress Cataloging-in-Publication Data

Wright, Wendy M.
    The time between: cycles and rhythms in ordinary time / Wendy
    M. Wright.
            p.   cm.
    Includes bibliographical references.
    ISBN 0-8358-0868-8
    1. Epiphany season-Prayer-books and devotions-English.
    2. Pentecost season-Prayer-books and devotions-English.
    I. Title.
    BV50.E7W75 1999
    242' .38-dc21   98-52414
                                                                 CIP
            Printed in the United States of America

For the
Families and Community
of Saint Cecilia's
Grade School and Parish,
Omaha, Nebraska

Contents

Acknowledgments   6

Preface   7

The Season of Ordinary Time   9

I.   Call and Response (Time after Epiphany)   17

At Water's Edge (First Week of Ordinary Time)   19
A Fresh Beginning (Mid-January)   29
The Lord's Day (Late January)   43
An Offering (Early February)   55
Good Gifts (Mid- to Late February)   67

II.   The Way That Lies Before (Time after Pentecost)   77

Three-in-One (Sunday after Pentecost)   79
God's Body (Second Week after Pentecost)   93
Gathered In (Late June)   106
Day by Day (Early July)   118
Much Has Been Forgiven (Late July to Early August)   132
Is There a Balm? (Late August)   145
Lifted Up (Mid-September)   155
Watching over Me (Late September to Early October)   167
Rising Like Incense (Late October)   183
Alpha and Omega (Early November)   201
With Me, before Me, behind Me
(Last Week of Ordinary Time)   221

Appendices: 225

Guide to Reading *The Time Between*   225
Table of the Liturgical Calendar (1999-2010)   230

Endnotes   231

ACKNOWLEDGMENTS

ANY BOOK, BUT ESPECIALLY A BOOK ABOUT THE LITURGICAL YEAR of the Christian churches, is not the sole creation of one author. It has its origins in the shared prayer of the community: in the hope, faith, and love of the generations whose lives have been sculpted by the gentle honing of the liturgy's primal rhythms. Thus this book must acknowledge both those historic persons whose words and prayers have nurtured me and those present-day persons with whom I have celebrated the church year. Gratitude is especially due to the communities at Saint Cecilia's Catholic Cathedral and school in Omaha, the Reverend Danny Morris of the Upper Room and the various ecumenical communities of the Academy for Spiritual Formation, and the Reverends Dick Junkin and Irv Moxley and the community in the Presbyterian Project for Congregational Spirituality.

More specifically, a debt of gratitude is owed to Father Dennis Hamm, S.J. and Father Joseph Weiss, S.J., of Creighton University's theology department who have been invaluable mentors in scripture and liturgical theology, respectively, and whose advice I relied upon in writing this book. Father Michael Proterra, S.J., dean of Creighton's College of Arts and Science, Father Richard Hauser, S.J., chair of the theology department, and Dr. Barbara Braden, graduate dean, are to be thanked for granting me the time and resources to complete the project. Jackie Lynch and Dr. Mary Kulhman spent hours helping with wordprocessing and manuscript changes. The publishing staff of The Upper Room, who first suggested that I write this book, also must be acknowledged. As must Robert Benson, whose attentive ear and resonant heart have been the book's best sounding board.

Preface

SAINT PAUL ENJOINED US TO "PRAY ALWAYS." THROUGHOUT THE varied periods of my life, in the different roles I have played—daughter, student, wife, mother, teacher, friend, spiritual guide, community member, global resident, scholar, writer—I have struggled to understand and then to live Paul's injunction, "Pray always." By this I don't believe Paul meant we are always to be "saying our prayers" but rather that our entire life must become infused with a spirit of prayerful awareness of God's presence, gifts, challenges, and call to us.

This attentive awareness is fostered in many ways: we read scripture, pray, worship, wait in silence, engage in works of justice and mercy, read devotional or theological works, and share our faith with others. These are significant means, but there is also the church year, the wonderful and ancient calendar by which the wider Christian community orders its life. It is, to my way of thinking, one of the most beautiful and inviting of Christian practices. One can enter into the life of Christ, the story of the church with its saints, and the astonishing mysteries we profess through the attentive celebration of the cycles and rhythms of the church year. Through it we become aware of the interpenetration of God in our collective and individual lives. If we really let this mystery penetrate our hearts, we not only pray, we become prayer. The great and central liturgical feasts of Christmas and Easter with their surrounding anticipatory and festive seasons (Advent, the days following Christmas through Epiphany, Lent, and the fifty days of the Easter Season through Pentecost) are familiar to most Christians. I have already written two books to accompany readers in these seasons.[1]

The time between the Christmas and Easter cycles is less familiar to many. Yet this two-part season is as rich a ground for prayer and as deep a spring for that attentive awareness as the great, strong seasons with which we are more familiar. I have written this modest guide to the time between, often known as "Ordinary Time," drawing inspiration from every quarter of the Christian communion, in its historical and contemporary denominational diversity with its myriad expressions. Throughout, I have woven in threads of the different cycles implicit in *The Time Between*—Sunday scriptures, daily readings, saints' feasts, the three varying synoptic portraits of Jesus—and explored these through the cumulative Christian wisdom that pertains to spiritual formation: hymns, poems, works of visual art, ritual and devotional practices, mystical and philosophical treatises.

The first segment of the book, "Call and Response," is meant to be reflected on during the days following Epiphany (January 6 or the nearest Sunday) until Ash Wednesday. The second section, "The Way That Lies Before," invites prayerful attentiveness in the days following Pentecost until the end of the church year in November. If desired, each chapter, which refracts the varying themes that emerge in *The Time Between*, may be read week by week by using the asterisk (★★★) breaks that punctuate them. An appendix at the book's end enables readers to have a more detailed sense of the book's structure and its relationship to the church calendar with its varied observances. I have also included a liturgical calendar for the years 1999-2010 for reference.

If time itself is a hallowed medium through which God meets us, and I think our faith affirms this, then the movement of the year with its cycles of months, days, hours, and minutes is a hallowed movement to which we might well become attuned. The church calendar opens our hearts and minds to this possibility. To "pray always" is to come alive to the reality of God-with-us in each season, even in the most ordinary of times.

The Season of Ordinary Time

IT DOES NOT MEAN WHAT YOU MIGHT THINK: BORING, UNEVENT-ful, undistinguished, everyday, ordinary. In fact, it means "counted time." The word *ordinary* comes from the word ordinal, to count. The liturgical season that occurs between the end of the extended Christmas season and the beginning of Lent and resumes again at Pentecost only to merge into Advent, is Counted Time. Many Christians, notably Episcopalians, Methodists, and Lutherans, may not even think of Ordinary Time as a distinct season, for on their calendars it often goes under the titles "time after Epiphany" and "time after Pentecost." In other quarters of Christendom, especially Roman Catholicism, the season is known as Ordinary Time.

Yet in some sense the season is "ordinary time" in the way you might think. An Episcopalian friend of mine, in response to my inquiries about the season's observance in his denomination, rolled his eyes. "We just get through it. There's so little cohesion to the readings: Hebrew Scriptures, the Epistles, the Gospels. What a relief to finally get to Advent where it coheres into a pattern, a recognizable thematic whole!" That is the impression many of us have. The strong seasons surrounding Christmas and Easter—Advent, Epiphany, Lent, Holy Week, the Easter season, Pentecost—are so vivid. Their distinctive violets, purples, and golds, their moods of sober introspection or trumpeted victory, their poinsettias and lilies, their haunting melodies—"Silent Night, Holy Night," "Were You There?"—their characteristic gestures of prostration or foot washing, their guiding stars, frankincense, far away hills or empty tombs, imprint the mysteries carried in these seasons firmly on our hearts.

Counted time holds us less closely. Except for its distinctive liturgical color—green—for most Christians Ordinary Time is simply in-between, filler in the year between the real seasons when the beauty of the faith is etched in high relief.

The truth is that as a liturgical season, Ordinary Time is very much like the ordinary, in-between times of our individual lives. Marked by occasional distinctive celebrations and remembrances, it is basically a time in which overarching yet more subtle rhythms, seasons and cycles predominate. In many of our lives there is a daily rhythm of rising, preparation, departure, arrival, energy expended in a variety of tasks, slowing down, and rest. This is punctuated by the usual rituals of eating, sleeping, the interactions with familiar friends, family, coworkers, and sometimes an encounter with someone new. In the process, the patterns of relationships, intimate or collegial, have their own dynamics of growth and development. We attend to business, shop, clean, maintain. Enveloping these daily rhythms are the terrestrial rhythms of sunrise, sunset, summer, fall, winter, and spring; the phases of the moon, of bodily change. Add to these the varied energies and incidents of the life cycle: the intimacy of young family ties, the adventurous explorations of youth, the mating and nesting of young adulthood, the providing and caretaking of parenthood, the honing of potential, the creativity of our labors, the generativity of later years, the surrender of the end.

So too with the liturgical season of Ordinary Time. It is a celebration of overlapping cycles and rhythms of all kinds. The most significant of these is the weekly cycle of Sundays. For the earliest Christians, Sunday was the original feast day. A feast was (and still is) a day given over to celebration, a time when practices and gestures appropriate to times of penance, like kneeling and fasting, were prohibited and when mysteries such as God-with-us, Christ-risen, and the Coming of the Spirit were celebrated with abundance and joy. Sunday was the time par excellence when Jesus' resurrection was commemorated. In the minds of the church fathers it was the "Lord's Day," and the "first day of creation." Long before the outlines of the now familiar calendar were sketched and enfleshed in practice, Sunday was the day most hallowed for Christians. Gradually, from the fourth century on, the day was designated as a time of rest and abstention from ordinary labor. Only much later was it overtly identified with the Jewish Sabbath. For us in the twentieth century all of these overlapping meanings still adhere to the first day of the week. Yet, for many, its fullness is still a matter for exploration. Its richness still waits our tasting.

After Sunday, the daily rhythm commands our attention next during Ordinary Time. Certainly the cycle of the day is both present and observed during the entire liturgical calendar but in counted time it, like the cycles of Sundays, comes into focus. For centuries Christians have punctuated the day with ritual prayer. They have sanctified time—made it holy—by setting aside periods for worship. They carve out windows in time through which eternity—God's time—is manifest. The most ancient pattern of gathered daily prayer within the Christian community was morning and evening observance, usually on market days when people were in the city. The classic forms of prayers were the psalms, intercessions, and the Lord's Prayer. When not gathered, believers prayed psalms independently.

Gradually a formalized pattern of daily prayer emerged. In the Roman Church it is known as the Divine Office and the liturgical book that guides the Office, the Breviary. In other denominations it is known simply as Daily Prayer. In the Office, the psalmody for the days revolves on a standardized cycle, and certain psalms have for centuries been associated with particular times of day. Thus psalms of praise are prayed in the morning, and the "incense psalms" occur at evening vespers.[2] The point of it all, whatever its form, is the sanctification of the day, the rhythmic attention to the God who greets us upon waking, and cradles us at the close of each day.

Beyond the weekly and daily rhythms celebrated on Sundays and in the daily offices, the liturgies of Ordinary Time have another dynamic. During the Sundays of this season we read from one of the three synoptic Gospels—Matthew, Mark, or Luke. We begin again every three years and start over the cycle of reading. The focus in the scriptures, no matter which evangelist we turn to, is mainly upon the years of Christ's ministry. During the first segment of the season, following the Christmas cycle and up until Lent, we are made aware of the mission of Jesus. The Christmas season closes and Ordinary Time begins dramatically with Jesus' sojourn down to the Jordan to be baptized by John where the heavens open and he hears himself declared "beloved son." God's missioning mantle in the form of a dove descends. Then we ascend with Jesus to the Mount and listen once again to his sermons. The second segment of the season encourages us to consider our discipleship and the mission of the church. We ponder his parables and are witness to his healings. We travel the dusty roads of Judea and Galilee. The varied portraits of Jesus and our early ecclesial forebears as painted by Matthew, Mark, and Luke frame the Christian life in three differing ways. Who is this Jesus? What is his mission and message? What is it to follow? To walk in his footprints? To hear ourselves called beloved daughters and sons? To know ourselves as children of God? To be sent? Missioned? These are the questions laid before us in the season of Ordinary Time.

The invitation is clear. We must wrestle with having heard ourselves called, like Peter; like Paul; like Mary of Magdala. Like generations of Christians who have entered deeply enough into the drama of the scriptures to have allowed the threads of their lives to be incorporated into the fabric of the divine mystery through the weaving of the liturgy. We are called to be both more than we ordinarily are and what we are, in fact, created to be holy, saints.

This wonderful season of Ordinary Time poses the questions for us: Will we follow? What will that following look like? The season also allows us the opportunity to celebrate the lives of others in our shared heritage who have responded to those questions with vigor and creative zest. All Christians in one way or another celebrate those whom we call saints. The Roman, Episcopal, Lutheran, and Methodist churches have fairly elaborate calendars for these saintly commemorations. The liturgical cycle of saints' days, known as the sanctoral cycle, is not confined to counted time. But it is during that time, when the intense momentum of the strong, extended cycles of Christmas and Easter are not arresting our attention, that we are perhaps freer to be attentive to the stories of the saints who have lived among us and who witness to the extraordinary diversity and creativity of transfigured life. Each of the Christian denominations thinks a little differently about saints. Whether they are considered simply those in the gathered church whose holiness is an inheritance that adheres to their baptism or whether saints are seen as the meritorious among those in Christ's body who in death form an intermediary link between the living and the divine, all Christians have some idea of saints and sanctity. And most denominations celebrate the stories of the saintly who have lived among us.

Ordinary Time is punctuated with other memorials and celebrations. Some of these are connected with the life cycle: birth, coming of age, marriage, death. Generally these rites of passage are celebrated within the Christian community with the rituals of baptism, confirmation, marriage, and the funeral rite. Other initiation rites such as ordination, reconciliation, or services of healing also punctuate our communal lives. And threading through the year is the primal ritual of communion. Our theologies and practices of Eucharist differ somewhat according to the Christian denomination of which we are a part. But we share more than we do not share.

Beyond these primary ritual structures, Christians of all denominations share other common celebrations. Together we observe Trinity Sunday. And during the last month of the church year, November, we enter together into an experience of end times, last things, even death. The solemnity of All Saints Day inaugurates the year's last month. Scripture proclamations are drawn from the Revelation to John or from Gospel segments that fore-shadow the Last Judgment and the ultimate fulfillment of the created order. The entire season closes with the celebration of Christ the King.

The cycles and seasons in which we are engaged during the liturgical season of Ordinary Time are both outward and inward. We participate in the ever-changing, cyclical patterns of the nat-ural seasons: spring's fresh promise, summer's sun-drenched play, fall's succulent harvest, winter's elegant austerity. We dance as well within the seasons of our personal and intergenerational lives: childhood's innocence, youth's irrepressible expansiveness, the courting and nesting of early adulthood, the labors of the householding and career years, the gracious generativity of older adulthood, the gentle relinquishment and waning of the last years. Each of these has its own outward and inward texture, its own psychological as well as its own spiritual tasks.

Similarly, we respond to the rhythms of our lives in faith. In-teriorly, we grow and change, for as spiritual beings we are not static. Spiritual writers of many centuries and from various branches of Christendom have spoken of this inner process in varied ways. John Bunyan, the seventeenth-century Puritan writer, imaged the changes geographically. He drew in word pic-tures a road map of the pilgrim's progress. John Climacus in the sixth century made the ladder his metaphor with which to artic-ulate the process of divine ascent. And the sixteenth-century Spanish mystic, Teresa of Avila, spoke of an interior castle with its many mansions and of a deepening, spiral-like progress to the center of the edifice. Tradition provides us with many metaphors.

Often the classics of our spiritual heritage speak of this inner process as the elimination of vices and the acquisition of virtue. These classics speak of the necessity of a means—discipline and prayer—through which that process is facilitated. They speak of our becoming transformed, of conversion, of being born anew, of transfiguration, of the labor of restoring the wounded, tarnished image of God within each of us. Ordinary Time creates a window on the long, slow, developmental process of this restoration. Intertwined with normal, psychological maturation, the process of inner transformation is nevertheless not synonymous with developmental dynamics. Although Christian denominations offer differing perspectives on the question, in general, spiritual growth is traditionally conceived as a matter of human activity elicited and aided by grace. To move in response to the Spirit's prompting is both to realize our innate potential and to be teased into something greater than what is possible in our own little lives. During this lengthy season of the church year we are thus invited to become attentive to the call of discipleship both outer and inner. What are we called to do? What work? With whom? Where? But also: What are we called to be? What habits and dispositions are we asked to relinquish? What qualities are we invited to cultivate?

I like to think of the entire spectrum of the liturgical cycle of Ordinary Time with all its varied rhythms—of Sunday observance, daily prayer, the sanctoral cycle, the tapestry of stories that dramatize the call and response of Jesus and the first disciples, the seasons of our own discipleship throughout the life cycle, the ritual practice of the great Christian rites, the dynamics of our inner faith lives—as one greater movement of desire to be face-to-face, heart-to-heart with God. The deep grammar of the church year's Ordinary Time is perhaps uttered most keenly in our ceaseless longing. By it we are propelled into the future. We pine for it as past. We trace the surface of the present with anxious fingertips. Call our desire awareness, mindfulness, mysticism, aesthetic sensitivity, faithfulness, or whatever. It is the fundamental movement of the Christian life.

Some of the earliest archeological evidence we have of the symbols that expressed the fullness of the Christian proclamation are inscriptions and bas—reliefs of the Alpha and the Omega. First and last. Beginning and end. This is the fundamental experience Christians have of the everyday search. Finally, it is a returning, a recognition, a meeting and being met, a being fully known.

> *We shall not cease from exploration*
> *And the end of all our exploring*
> *Will be to arrive where we started*
> *And know the place for the first time.*[3]

I.

CALL AND RESPONSE

(Time after Epiphany)

[One night Eli] . . . was lying down in his usual place, while Samuel slept in the temple of the LORD where the Ark of God was. Before the lamp of God had gone out, the LORD called him, and Samuel answered, "Here I am!" and ran to Eli, saying "You called me: here I am." "No, I did not call you; lie down again." So he went and lay down. The LORD called Samuel again, and he got up and went to Eli. "Here I am," he said; "surely you called me." "I did not call, my son," he answered; "lie down again." Now Samuel had not yet come to know the LORD, and the word of the LORD had not been disclosed to him. When the LORD called him for the third time, he again went to Eli and said, "Here I am; you did call me." Then Eli understood that it was the LORD calling the child; he told Samuel to go and lie down and said, "If he calls again, say, 'Speak, LORD; thy servant hears thee.'" So Samuel went and lay down in his place.

The LORD came and stood there, and called, "Samuel, Samuel," as before.

As Samuel grew up, the LORD was with him, and none of his words went unfulfilled.

(I SAMUEL 3: 2–10, 19, NEB)

At Water's Edge

(First Week of Ordinary Time)

Wade in the water,
Wade in the water, children,
Wade in the water,
God's a gonna trouble the water.

Look over yonder, what do I see?
God's a gonna trouble the water;
The Holy Ghost a coming on me,
God's a gonna trouble the water.[4]

IT BEGINS WITH WATER. CHAOS OR CREATION. BIRTH OR RE-birth. Out of the waters comes life, new life. All emerges from water. So too with Ordinary Time. The last liturgical celebration of the extended Christmas season is the feast—the festive commemoration—of the baptism of the Lord. It is the primal feast of water. Jesus goes down to the Jordan to be baptized by John and there, river water sloshing at his thighs, Jesus is initiated. And Jesus initiates as well. He inaugurates the rite of water baptism, the rite that stands at the headwaters of the sacramental streams of new life that the Christian faith promises. John the evangelist gives us a bird's-eye view of the scene on the Jordan's banks two thousand years ago.

[John] saw Jesus coming towards him. "Look," he said, "There is the Lamb of God; it is he who takes away the sin of the world. This is he of whom I spoke when I said, "After me a man is coming who takes rank before me"; for before I was born, he already was. I myself

did not know who he was; but the very reason why I came, baptizing in water, was that he might be revealed to Israel."

John testified further: "I saw the Spirit coming down from heaven like a dove and resting upon him. I did not know him, but he who sent me to baptize in water had told me, "When you see the Spirit coming down upon someone and resting upon him, you will know that this is he who is to baptize in Holy Spirit." I saw it myself, and I have borne witness. This is God's chosen One.

(JOHN 1: 29-34, NEB)

The evangelist underscores for us the extraordinary nature of the event. We meet a man, Jesus, who ventures out with the Galilean crowds in response to the Baptist's inflammatory preaching. Presumably to the ordinary observer there is nothing notable about this Jesus, an unexceptional carpenter from Nazareth. But John recognizes him as exceptional. He is the Chosen One, the Christ, the one on whom the Spirit has settled, into whom God's own power is breathed.

On one level this story played out at the river's edge is a theological one. We learn of the divine inspiration that resides in this carpenter. We hear him proclaimed as the Anointed. Other translations of the text make us aware that he is the Son of God. He is the *beloved* son, the synoptic writers tell us. On another level, the story of the Lord's baptism is an ecclesial one. The Christian churches harken back to this event as the prototype for the sacrament of initiation into the community. In baptism we enter into the lived experience of the faith that emerges from the cleansing, healing, and generative waters of life. On still another level, the spiritual, this story has yet a third meaning. It is a sign and a visible image of the newness, the fresh beginning, into which we are each invited. For the gospel stories are not simply stories of God or of the church or of abstract truths holy and sublime. They are stories that reflect to us the truths of our own lives. They are mirrors we hold up to see our own images refracted. They are stories that tell us who we are and instruct us about whom we might become.

The story of the baptism in the Jordan is thus our story as well as it is that of Jesus the carpenter from Nazareth. On this level it is a story about our foundational identity. In the variant of the story narrated by the Gospel writers Matthew, Mark, and Luke, we learn that in midimmersion, Jesus, dove fluttering round his head, is addressed by a mysterious, heavenly voice. "You are my Son, the Beloved; with you I am well pleased" (Luke 3:22), the voice announces. He is called son, God's own child. Not only that, he is also called beloved. In these simple words is encoded the most foundational truth of the spiritual life. We are God's children, created in the divine image and likeness, and we are beloved.

It is not clear to me that most of us genuinely grasp this deep truth. Lurking in most people are feelings of inadequacy, shame, guilt, and uncertainty. Nor have most of us clarified for ourselves the crucial distinctions between what others think of us, what we do, and what we are. These are, in fact, quite distinct realities. At bottom, we simply are. Our being, as created children of God, has infinite worth. Whether we live up to our intrinsic dignity is another issue. Sometimes what we do does not reflect the truth of our being. And we should rightfully be accountable for our actions and feel appropriate chagrin or remorse when we are remiss. But this is not the same as feeling shame for merely being. Nor should our failures trigger a sense of worthlessness in us. Some of us also confuse our sense of self with the opinions others hold of us. Our families and friends, the neighbors, our peer groups, our bosses, or coworkers become the mirrors held up to behold ourselves. Their admiration or disdain shapes our opinion of who we are.

Many American Christians have gained an awareness of the way this process is operative in popular culture. Teenaged girls starve themselves because they cannot achieve the wraithlike standard of beauty held up in the media; middle-class men who have formed their sense of being through their careers become suicidal when they are laid off. What we do and how we look to others become the yardsticks for measuring ourselves. These are obvious examples. But the process can be much more subtle and can affect us deeply in our spiritual lives. We may have built a strong sense of spiritual self-worth because we have always followed the rules of our church, and we may look at the rule breakers who share the pews with us with thinly veiled condescension. We might be like the Pharisee, puffed up with our own righteousness, praying in gratitude that we are not like that wicked publican. Or we may believe, deep down, that we are not worthy because we are one of those rule-breakers or we are one whose ideas differ from the majority. The love and acceptance of our families and faith communities are important, even essential, components of our spiritual lives. But they are not identical with (although they may help us find) the deep knowledge of our belovedness as God's children.

Thomas Merton, perhaps the most well-known Catholic spiritual writer of the twentieth century, was clear that sorting out these distinctions was an essential part of the spirit journey. Merton wrote of the "false self" and the "true self" in his efforts to describe the subtle, illusions with which we are burdened.

> Every one of us is shadowed by an illusory person: a false self.
>
> This is the [person] that I want myself to be but who cannot exist, because God does not know anything about [it]. . . .
>
> My false and private self is the one who wants to exist outside the radius of God's will and God's love—outside of reality and outside of life. And such a self cannot help but be an illusion.
>
> We are not very good at recognizing illusions: least of all the ones we have about ourselves. . . .
>
> All sin starts from the assumption that my false self, the self that

*exists only in my own egocentric desires, is the fundamental reality
of life to which everything else in the universe is ordered. Thus I use
up my life trying to accumulate pleasures and experiences and power
and honor and knowledge and love, to clothe this false self and construct its nothingness into something objectively real. . . .*

*But there is no substance under the things I have gathered around
me. . . . when they are gone there will be nothing left of me but my
own nakedness and emptiness and hollowness. . . .*

*Ultimately the only way that I can be myself is to become iden-
tified with Him in Whom is hidden the reason and fulfillment of my
existence . . . If I find Him, I will find myself and if I find my true
self I will find Him . . . .*

*There exists some point at which I can meet God in a real and
experimental contact . . . it is the point where my . . . being depends
upon His love.*[5]

This is the "point" where self-knowledge as beloved children
is born: the point where our being is discovered to depend and
rest in God's love. We may know our belovedness as an intellec-
tual construct. We may be able to repeat the phrase, "For God so
loved the world . . ." but we may have no deep personal knowledge of that fact. In my experience working with people, I have
found that it is sometimes easier to grasp this truth from other
than a subjective viewpoint. Sometimes we get a glimpse into the
nature of God's love for us by attending to things outside ourselves.

★   ★   ★

In the fall of 1997 I had the opportunity to do research on my
sabbatical project in France. While in Paris, I convinced my traveling companion to take a short break from our academic labors
and visit the gardens at Giverny where the impressionist painter
Claude Monet had lived and worked in the early years of the

century. Giverny is something of a favorite spot for American tourists yet the property is far enough away from Paris to give the visitor a sense of the bucolic idyll that so attracted the painter. Monet's cottage with its Dutch-blue kitchen and sunshine-yellow dining room, its magnificent light-filled atelier, and its astonishing collection of Japanese prints, sits at the front of an extended property that splays out from behind the cottage in a riot of blooms and bowers, trellises and leaf-covered arcades. We saw the gardens in late September yet they still were vivid with the russets, oranges, blood-reds and fuchsias of late-flowering plants. Further back still on the property lies Monet's famous water-lily pond. In his time he must have crossed a dirt-lined country path to gain access to the pond. Today visitors cross under the country highway through a specially constructed tunnel that leads to a short series of steps, guiding one onto the meandering pathways that surround the rather elongated pond. Monet's love of the Japanese aesthetic is evident, for the comfortable provincial charm of the French countryside is there blended with the artful poise of a Zen garden. There is an arched footbridge, an occasional seated bench, curves and inlets that invite contemplation. The attentive stillness of the landscape envelopes visitors who stroll, linger, stop to snap a picture, or merely behold the fields of lilies lightly suspended on the pond's surface. Monet's gardens were a delight to experience.

But it was not until we returned to Paris that the gardens were transfigured for me. It happened quite unexpectedly and without any calculation. On our way to visit a church that was on our academic itinerary, my colleague and I stopped at the Musée de l'Orangerie, a museum that houses the works of several of the Impressionist painters. We perused the floor plan in the museum brochure and learned that the lower level of the Orangerie is given over to Monet's monumental series, *Water Lilies*. I was intrigued to see the paintings, in part because we had just been to Giverny but also because I had seen reproductions of portions of the series. We toured the upper floors of Renoirs and Picassos and headed down to the lower level. I was not prepared for what I found there. At the entry to the oval-shaped galleries, of which there are two, was an explanation of the genesis of the *Water Lilies* series. The occasion was the armistice that ended World War I, the "war to end all wars." Monet by that time was a legend, the patriarch of France's artistic community. The series was a gift to France itself, to its people. The gift was—I'm not sure how to put this—Monet's eyes.

I had been to the pond at Giverny on a fall afternoon and lux-uriated in its beauty. But Monet had lived with those lilies, lov-ingly walked those paths and, most important, gazed upon that place with eyes of love. When he laid brush to canvas he gave to the world, in the wake of Armageddon, a vision of creation transfigured in and by its own being. The series, in eight monu-mental panels wrapped around the walls of the oval galleries, captures the infinitely varied visage of the lilies bathed in the changing lights of morning, evening, spring, summer, autumn, and winter.

I wept. What Monet saw he gave to the world. He saw the in-finite beauty of the most ordinary of things—a water-lily pond. He saw the dynamism and variability in objects that many of us would regard as generic: lilies and water. But Monet saw that each lily in each season at each time of day was an irrepeatable astonishment. In the particular, in the concrete, in the finite, in-finite wonder is beheld.

I will claim this, knowing it is merely an analogy: what Monet saw when he gazed on his water lilies, God must see when be-holding creation. Irrepeatable astonishment. Infinity coded in a single leaf. Eternity uttered in the late hour of a summer's after-noon. Beloved.

What Monet saw, Jesus heard as he stood ankle deep in the cleansing waters of the Jordan. "You are my Beloved." And this is the self-knowledge to which we each are called.

I suspect we have an innate, inarticulate knowing of this coded in our cells, stamped from the very beginning on our hearts—an inborn consciousness of what Merton calls the "true self." But we have forgotten, or have become incapable of recognizing it. For a thousand reasons. Perhaps it is original sin. Or a failure of parental nurturance. Or the moral vacuum of a society that provides no context for such a sacred intuition. For whatever reasons, we so often cannot find our way back to that primal intuition. And that, I think, is where baptism comes in. Whatever our theological perspective on baptism as a rite within the community of faith, the primordial rite of entering into the waters speaks of a renewal so profound that we are washed clean of all that would obscure that truest knowing of our selves. Bathed in the gentle waters of being beloved. Tenderly stripped to the barest and most beautiful of original innocence.

Our two eldest children, both daughters, were baptized at the Old Mission Church in Santa Barbara. The Mission, one of an elongated strand of Spanish colonial architectural gems that stretch the length of the California coast along El Camino Real, the ancient "royal highway," is an astonishment of a structure. Despite much reconstruction undertaken in the wake of earthquakes and fires, the "Queen of the Missions" remains an almost pristine example of the vigorous hybrid born of the Spanish baroque and Native Amerindian artistic sensibilities. Thick, adobe-red walls shield the sanctuary from the hot, arid sun. On the interior walls, cloud-lofted madonnas that could have been painted by Murillo or Valasquez and the writhing, blood-soaked crucifixes so characteristic to Spanish Catholicism, coexist with the stark geometric pictographs one would expect to find adorning the walls of an Indian cave tucked away in the hills above the coast.

On the right side of the sanctuary, as one enters the Mission's oversized wooden doors, is the ancient baptistry. It was there, in that small space, cooled by the sheltering adobe and the sheltering presence of loved ones huddled around an antique marble fount, on quiet afternoons in January and July, that our daughters were initiated into the most primal of Christian rituals.

Baptism is many things. An act of cleansing. New birth. Incorporation into a community of faith. An entrustment of a child to that community and especially to the parents and godparents. It is a call. A naming. The child is given an identity. This child is beloved. This child is acknowledged as a daughter or son of God.

Recently, I had occasion to telephone an acquaintance about the business of an academic society to which we both belong. He is a man I had met perhaps twice, always in the context of meetings which provided little opportunity to communicate about anything but professional matters. In the midst of our phone conversation, he suddenly questioned me. "You have children, don't you?" "Yes, three," I responded. "Well," he spoke rather intently, "I just came from dropping our only daughter off for her first day of kindergarten." My acquaintance didn't have to say much more. We exchanged parent talk about the half-proud, half-teary experience of that oh-so-ordinary and absolutely monumental rite of passage—the first day of school. A passage full of anticipation and some fear for children, but a passage even more powerful for parents. Just as the conception and births of our children, especially our first children, are initiatory events of vast magnitude, so the first school day is one of a long string of initiations we will undergo into the poignant and painful spiritual arts of welcoming and letting go that are so fundamental to family life. Through our children we are birthed over and over again into the fearful wonder of unconditional love. We nurture, instruct, and guide our little ones but we also relinquish them, little by little, to their ultimate freedom and to the mystery of a world that only rarely regards them with the eyes of love. Our initiation into the fullness of parental love is gradual. Our birth process lifelong. It parallels that other profound lifelong initiation, our own gradual awakening to the truth of God's gaze as it rests upon us.

If the baptism of Jesus brings closure to the Christmas cycle and provides the setting upon which the succeeding liturgical season of ordinary time rests, so too our baptisms set the stage for the succeeding drama of our spiritual lives. We pause at the water's edge. We are marked with a sign of faith, encircled by a cloud of witnesses, immersed in a story, deep and wide in its proportions. We rise out of the waters to a new birth. And we each hear ourselves named—beloved son, beloved daughter, of God.

A Fresh Beginning

(Mid-January)

Morning has broken
Like the first morning
Blackbird has spoken
Like the first bird
Praise for the singing!
Praise for the morning!
Praise for them springing
Fresh from the Word![6]

I REMEMBER AS A GRADE-SCHOOLER IN LOS ANGELES, WAKING
each morning to the hope of a new day. My parents and I lived
on the downside of a hill overlooking the sprawling metropolis
in the Silverlake district of central Los Angeles. My bedroom had
a full-length glass window that looked out on the leafy foliage of
a mock orange tree. Although I did not have a full view of the
low-lying city basin (I would have to go upstairs to the living
room above my room for that), from my window I could see a
bit of the extended city and a vast expanse of sky framed by fragrant, dark-green foliage. Each day, waking to the morning sunlight streaming across my blue coverlet, was a new beginning. I
remember especially the sense of anticipation, of innate hope,
that welled up as I contemplated the hours stretching before me.
It was a different feeling from other sorts of anticipation—like
Christmas or a birthday. (Those exciting feelings were more particular and, strangely, more doomed to frustration or disappoint-
ment. Even the best birthday was soon over. The Christmas
presents and the family dinner were marvelous but the anticipa-

tion had a hungry, agitated feel to it.) The anticipation I felt at the dawn of each day was distinctive. Buoyant, more generalized, an instinctive tapping into the sheer grace of life itself. I knew, no matter how difficult the previous day, no matter how tired or overwrought I had been, that the light of morning would bring with it a renewed vigor and a changed perspective. A fresh beginning. Adulthood has not always provided mornings charged with the same vigor of those of my youthful years. Yet the fact remains that each day is a new beginning. Prayer awakens us to that reality. We are called into newness each day.

Abbot Poemen, one of those early Christians who fled the world and sought refuge in the deserts of Syria, Egypt, and Palestine in pursuit of the renewed and revigorated life, is remembered as saying, "Each day is a fresh beginning." From the earliest centuries, it has been a Christian practice to begin the day with prayer. Saint Paul enjoined the communities of faith to which he wrote to "pray always." By this he did not mean, I am quite certain, that they should simply engage in pious exercise or be forever seeking God's pardon. He implied, and subsequent generations of Christians have understood, that time itself must be sanctified, made holy.

If time is potentially a series of windows through which eternity might be glimpsed, then we would do well to open those windows. This means prying open whatever holds our awareness tightly clasped. Whatever form it takes—words, ritual gestures, songs, attentiveness, silence, stillness—prayer opens the windows of our hearts and minds. It hones our awareness of the moving, hovering presence that envelopes us always. It was, of course, a Jewish practice to greet each day with ritual prayer. Christians followed the same practice, I would presume, not simply because it was traditional but because the advent of each new day does in fact, as Abbot Poeman pointed out, mark a fresh beginning.

There are many types of prayer that have been taught and practiced in the church's history. One of the most enduring forms is liturgical prayer—the church's shared and common prayer. And among the earliest forms of common prayer is the daily liturgy of the morning. Its specific form has evolved over the centuries and at present it is variantly articulated in the many Christian denominations, but its basic components are stable.

It begins with an uttered declaration that dispels the silence of night.

> O God, open our lips,
> And we shall declare your praise.[7]
>
> (PSALM 51:15)

The liturgy begins with the intimation that we are designed for prayer, that our very lips and the words they form can be instruments of praise. Of all the creatures in this magnificent world, we are the ones who have the capacity for self-reflection and the ability to self-consciously speak forth what we are. We can sing of beauty, speak words that bring peace. Or we can do otherwise. Our speaking and our voicing is not simply reflective, it is substantive. It creates something new. We open our lips. We shape words that fling open a window in time and reveal that time is a thin veneer on the surface of eternity.

Christians have for centuries felt the Psalter to contain the most self-disclosive of words to reflect the divine goodness to itself. Certain psalms are cherished as morning songs of praise. Psalm 63 especially gives voice to the anticipation, sensed in the sweet freshness of dawn, that God's presence surrounds and envelops us.

> In the morning I will sing
> glad songs of praise to you.
>
> You are my God, I long for you
> from early in the morning

My whole being desires you
    like a dry, worn, waterless land,
My soul thirsts for you.

In the sanctuary
    let me see how mighty are your works;
Your constant love
    is better than life itself,
And so I will praise you.

I will give you thanks
    as long as I shall live;
I raise my hands in prayer,
    and my soul will feast and be filled,
And so I will sing and praise you.

As I lie in bed
    I remember you, O Lord;
I think of you all night long,
    for you are my constant help.

In the shadow of your wings,
    I sing for joy.
I cling to you,
    Your hand keeps me safe.[8]

God, who enfolds our little lives at each end, whose grace sustains us, whose felt presence is so sweet that life without it feels dry as dust, is a God of new beginnings. The God who is at once Alpha and Omega is so not only in the sense of being the source and end of our creation. We experience God's abundant, exuberant creativity whenever newness breaks through into our dust-drenched days. The in-breaking of freshness is structured into the very fabric of our world. We are invited into its tender promise, its rising hope, its renewed possibility with each dawn.

I suppose it is not surprising that from the early days of the faith, Christians have placed the biblical Canticle of Zachary within the liturgy of morning prayer. It is truly a hymn to fresh beginnings. Along with the psalms, several ancient canticles or songs found in scripture are used in the liturgies of daily prayer. Zachary's song is such a one. Early in the Gospel of Luke, in an atmosphere charged with anticipation and the promise of new life, we meet the priest, Zachary, husband of Elizabeth, and Mary's cousin. He and his wife were, as the text says, righteous in God's sight. But they grieved because they had no children and were both of advanced age. All this was changed when an angelic announcement prophesied the birth of a son. We learn that Zachary was skeptical of the prophecy and because of this, he was struck speechless. It was only with the birth of the promised child that his tongue was released. Rather than following the custom of naming him after his father, the couple named him John, and when the revelation was made to all the astonished as-sembled neighbors, Zachary opened his mouth and began prais-ing God. The beautiful hymnic words that came forth prophesied of another child, soon to be born in Bethlehem, of whom baby John would be the prophet.

Zachary's canticle is truly a song of the morning, full of an-ticipation of the wondrous redemption of the people Israel, of the transformation of the world into a place of peace. It sings of the tender mercies of a God who sends the daybreak to dispel the night and a shining child to illuminate the darkness.

Blessed be the Lord, the God of Israel,
  for he has looked favorably on his people and redeemed them.
He has raised up a mighty savior for us
  in the house of his servant David,
as he spoke through the mouth of his holy prophets from of old,

that we would be saved from our enemies and from the hand of
    all who hate us.
Thus he has shown mercy promised to our ancestors,
    and has redeemed his holy covenant,
the oath he swore to our ancestor Abraham,
    to grant us that we, being rescued from the hands of our enemies,
might serve him without fear, in holiness and righteousness
    before him all our days.
And you, child, will be called the prophet of the Most High;
    for you will go before the Lord to prepare his ways,
to give knowledge of salvation to his people
    by the forgiveness of their sins.
By the tender mercy of our God,
    the dawn from on high will break upon us,
to give light to those who sit in darkness and in the shadow of death,
    to guide our feet into the way of peace.

(LUKE 1:68-79)

God is a God of fresh beginnings. Of dawn. Of new life. Of a transfigured world where the most poignant language lodged in the human heart will be fulfilled. The dawn of which Zachary sings is utterly unique. But the advent of each day's rising dawn, while unique in its particularity, is a continual advent suitable for ordinary time, a fresh beginning that arrives with the earth's own cyclical rhythms. We greet it with prayer.

★   ★   ★

While the liturgical movements of daily prayer awaken us to the possibility of newness, so the cumulative spiritual tradition awakens us to the same possibility in a different way. For Christianity is above all a religion concerned with making things new—new wineskins, new covenant, new life, new birth, new song. Our imaginations are primed to anticipate not only the blush of daylight or the renewal of lost humanity or the renovation of the cosmos, we are poised to expect personal renewal. We hope, we ask for, and we expect newness for ourselves. We call it conversion.

The stories of the first Christians are above all, tales of conversion, of a radical change of perspective that initiates a new life. Perhaps the most archetypal of conversions is that of Saul—known later, of course, as Paul—whose dramatic encounter with the risen Christ forever altered his destiny.[9] Artists, exegetes, and preachers have through the centuries imagined Saul, fierce persecutor of the nascent followers of "the Way," astride his steed, flung to the ground by the force of the encounter. The scriptural accounts do not suggest that the unwary traveler was on a horse, but they do save for us an astonishingly dramatic account. In fact, we have three variants of the event each appearing at significant intervals preserved in the Book of Acts. Twice, Paul himself is the first-person narrator. In the first of these he defends himself against the accusations by the Jewish community in Jerusalem.

Brothers and fathers, listen to the defense that I now make before you. . . . I am a Jew, born in Tarsus in Cilicia, but brought up in this city at the feet of Gamaliel, educated strictly according to our ancestral law, being zealous for God, just as all of you are today. I persecuted this Way up to the point of death by binding both men and women and putting them in prison, as the high priest and the whole council of elders can testify about me. From them I also received letters to the brothers in Damascus, and I went there in order to bind those who were there and to bring them back to Jerusalem for punishment.

While I was on my way and approaching Damascus, about noon a great light from heaven suddenly shone about me. I fell to the ground and heard a voice saying to me, "Saul, Saul, why are you persecuting me?" I answered, "Who are you, Lord?" Then he said to me, "I am Jesus of Nazareth whom you are persecuting." Now those who were with me saw the light but did not hear the voice of the one who was speaking to me. I asked, "What am I to do, Lord?" The Lord said to me, "Get up and go to Damascus; there you will be told everything that has been assigned to you to do." Since I could not see because of the brightness of that light, those who were with me took my hand and led me to Damascus.

(ACTS 22:1–11)

Saul/Paul's conversion was swift and dramatic, a being taken unaware. It was an experience of divine in-breaking into the clouded and cluttered reality that has no room for God. This type of decisive, singular encounter is not unfamiliar in the annals of Christian history. Desert ascetics of the fourth through seventh centuries and their later medieval monastic counterparts preserved a genre of legend that has become known as tales of "harlots in the desert." They tell of women of questionable repute—courtesans and actresses mainly—who are swiftly converted from their former lives by hearing a word of scripture or by some contact with a saintly man. It takes a bit of suspension of our twentieth-century sensibilities to grasp the spiritual points of these stories and to set aside our concerns about negative stereotyping of women. Yet when we understand that "fallen women" were in their ancient cultures symbols for all that was lost in the world—sensuality, corruption, decadence, self-preoccupation—the stories make sense. For these women were swiftly and absolutely converted to lives of heroic sanctity (some are shown becoming famous desert ascetics) simply by the power of the Word or the witness of a saintly life. The tales functioned as moral cautionary tales to zealous would-be saints who, puffed up with their own ascetic exploits, could easily forget that the power of transformation proceeds not from themselves but from the divine initiative. The harlot stories speak of sin and grace, the gratuitousness of redemption, and the merciful love of God for the fallen world. Not all swift-conversion stories in the tradition are so picturesque, but they all forcefully convey the idea that divine power subverts the order of things as they are to inaugurate something fresh and new.

Possibly the evangelical tradition is the one among the varieties of Christian communities that has most emphasized the experience of a singular conversion. While there is within the broad stream of evangelical spirituality itself a variety of ways that conversion is treated, in general it is safe to say that "conversion is the crisis of the soul in which it turns to God."[10] Characteristic of that tradition is the story of George Whitefield, the notable eighteenth-century preacher whose persuasive oratory inflamed a generation of English citizens.[11] Whitefield grew up, the seventh son of prosperous innkeepers in Gloucester, assuming he would become a clergyman. His dramatic aptitudes, his skill at elocution, and his vivid imagination all revealed themselves at an early age. As he approached adulthood, he embarked on a rigorous regime of ascetic discipline that damaged his health and left him anxious and depressed. Whitefield was rescued from his gloom when, during his convalescence, he was filled with the joy of assurance and forgiveness.

God was pleased to remove the heavy load . . . O with what joy . . . joy that was full of and big with glory, was my soul filled, when the weight of sin went off, and an abiding sense of the pardoning love of God and a full assurance of faith, broke in on my disconsolate soul.[12]

For the young man, this experience of conversion was a gratuitous gift of God, one that changed him forever. No longer would he, or for that matter anyone who was so seized by grace, be the same, either before God or in the inner life.

As it may be said of a piece of gold, that was once in the ore, after it has been cleansed, purified and polished, that it is a new piece of gold; as it may be said of a bright glass that has been covered over with filth, when it is wiped, and so become transparent and clear, that it is a new glass; . . . so our souls, though still the same as to essence, yet are so purged, purified and cleansed from their natural dross . . . by the blessed influence of the holy Spirit, that they may be properly said to be made anew.[13]

This quintessential conversion experience of once and for all having the burden of sin lifted off one's shoulders, this vivifying experience of beginning anew, is a hallmark of evangelical spirituality. It could give birth to prayer, to thanksgiving, and most especially, to song. It was the great hymn writer Charles Wesley, brother of John and cofounder with his sibling of the eighteenth-century renewal movement within the Church of England that became known as Methodism, who composed the words that celebrate the experience of conversion, of return to God.[14] Wesley's early hymnbook was not simply a collection of religious songs, it was a musical recapitulation of the spiritual life, a sort of melodic *Pilgrim's Progress* with the geographical itinerary of the pilgrim Christian transposed into lyric and melody. There was a hymn for every inner movement of the spiritual life as well as for liturgical moments, times of day, and specific gatherings. Wesley called it a "little body of experimental and practical divinity."[15]

Wesley celebrated the experience of conversion in his classic hymn, which is still sung today.

> *Oh, for a thousand tongues to sing*
> *My dear Redeemer's praise!*
> *The glories of my God and King,*
> *The triumphs of his grace!*

My gracious Master, and my God,
  Assist me to proclaim,
To spread through all the earth abroad
  The honors of thy name.

Jesus, the name that charms our fears,
  That bids our sorrows cease-
'Tis music in the sinner's ears,
  'Tis life, and health, and peace.

He breaks the power of canceled sin,
  He sets the prisoner free;
His blood can make the foulest clean-
  His blood availed for me.

Hear him, ye deaf; his praise, ye dumb,
  Your loosened tongues employ;
Ye blind, behold your Savior come,
  And leap, ye lame, for joy!

Look unto him, ye nations, own
  Your God, ye fallen race;
Look, and be saved through faith alone,
  Be justified by grace.

See all your sins on Jesus laid:
  The Lamb of God was slain,
His soul was once an offering made
  For every soul of man.

. . . .

With me, your chief, ye then shall know,
  Shall feel your sins forgiven;

Anticipate your heaven below,
And own that love is heaven.[16]

★   ★   ★

In other corners of the Christian world the conversion experience, while very real, is nonetheless depicted much less dramatically. The return to God, while it sometimes manifests itself in moments of operatic intensity, is conceptualized more often as a slow and continual process—rather like the laborious incremental shift in direction that a giant ocean vessel completes than the swift pivot of a jackrabbit. Conversion is a lifelong process of honing in the direction of the divine or a gradual, onionlike peeling away of the layers of deception that prevent us from realizing our true selves.

The desert dwellers of the faith's early centuries pursued the spiritual life in such an incremental way. On occasion their departures from "the world" were dramatic. The prototypical desert figure, Antony of Egypt, gave up all his worldly possessions, including the guardianship of his younger sister, and retreated to the remote countryside far from his native village after hearing a sermon on Jesus' command to the young man to sell all he had, give his money to the poor, and follow.[17] Once the retreating ascetics arrived at their destinations they set about the long labor of conversion, the slow, vigilant stripping away of the false self shaped by the "world" from which they had fled and an uncovering of the true self, the image of God in Christ. Antony's story, recorded for posterity by the Alexandrian bishop Athanasius, shows us a wild warrior of a man doing solitary battle with the demons of luxury, pride, greed, and self-aggrandizement and conquering them through the mysterious power of Christ.

Antony and his like fled to the desert not simply to withdraw from the forces of the world, but because they knew the desert to be a fecund place. Silent and solitary, life in the wilderness of

Egypt, Palestine, and Syria was transformative. The vast emptiness of space was a creative matrix, the deafening silence a forge
that could hammer out a new and transformed humanity.

I love the stories of Antony and the other desert dwellers, for
they speak to me of the power of silent sacred spaces and of the
primal longing that courses through the bloodstreams of generations of Christians, a longing to be reborn, renewed, made
fresh, to begin once again at the beginning and see it for the first
time. And I think of the years of my childhood when my parents, in the middle of winter, would take me to the deserts of
Southern California. Winters when we were growing up in the
Los Angeles basin were never the health haven that envious
snowbound friends might imagine. I was plagued as a child with
recurrent respiratory illness and, despairing of my ever recover-
ing from a chronic cold or cough, midwinter my parents would
pack up, take me out of school, and head for Palm Springs and
the El Poco Lodge. Palm Springs in the fifties was not the ex-
clusive resort that it was subsequently to become. Instead, it was
a fairly sleepy hamlet dotted with modest, private residences and
a few lodges and small-scale hotels.

The El Poco Lodge was our traditional haunt. It lay on the
outskirts of the small village, a pleasant walk toward the foothills
from what was then the center of the town. Of the town, I remember the mom-and-pop candy store, the retail merchants,
shops lined with racks of coarse, stringy leather bolo ties and the
bouffant swirls of square-dance dresses, the sidewalk art sales
where local retirees hawked the olive and beige oil paintings of
desertscapes they had crafted in the long, unhurried hours of
their afternoons. And I recall the warmth of evening walks when
daylight heat still hung in the sweet, dry air and bright luminaria
cast light necklaces of yellow-green beads along the edges of
passing lawns.

But mostly I remember the silence of the desert, a silence so
palpable it enveloped and muffled any sound that tried to chal-

lenge its mighty weight. El Poco Lodge was at the far end of one of the streets that wandered out the distant end of town. A small hostel with perhaps a dozen motel-style rooms edging the swimming pool and another half dozen housekeeping units scattered back on the property at the base of the desert foothills, the lodge was unpretentious, yet the enormous power of its venue lent it great prestige. A tiny utility kitchen abutting a brightly painted breakfast nook looked out on a small grove of lemon trees from which hung yellow citrus the size of grapefruits. Beyond the miracle lemons the rugged slope of the foothills ascended, beyond that in one direction the steepening slopes, in the other, the open expanse of desert floor.

Never let anyone tell you the desert is barren. It is teeming with life. Agile reptilian creatures lurked under stones, tenacious plants clung to life in the thin, sandy topsoil, minute wildflowers, nearly invisible unless viewed from close range, dotted the desert floor. All of it was cradled in the vast embrace of a silence so deep it calmed all thought and feeling. Life in the palm desert pulsed without all the rustle and restless sounds of wind, trees, oceans, or rivers. My parents brought me to the desert in the wintertime, ostensibly to absorb the sunshine, to let the dry air of the arid landscape leech into lungs and sinuses. Lying wrapped in a light blanket on the deserted poolside deck I did indeed receive the healing of the desert climate. But in the process, the deep silence entered me and taught me to listen, to see, to hear, to become attentive to the noiseless substrata beneath all that is.

Conversion, the desert ascetics assure us, is forged in such a place, a place of listening awareness where one becomes attentive to the silence of God. There, in the vast stillness of desert solitude, we are gradually converted, unmade, and remade. We become a fresh beginning.

The Lord's Day

(Late January)

Praise to the Lord, the Almighty,
*   the king of creation!*
O my soul, praise him,
*   for he is your health and salvation!*
Come, all who hear:
*   Brothers and sisters, draw near,*
Praise him in glad adoration.[18]

MY NOTIONS ABOUT SUNDAY ARE COLORED NOT ONLY BY MY experience but also by my literary excursions into the American folkstories found in books like Laura Ingalls Wilder's Little House series. Etched in my memory is the tale told by Pa of his own father's childhood and his strict Puritan Sabbath keeping. Sundays were observed in America past as days of absolute solemnity. No reading other than the Bible, no recreation, certainly no loud talking, playing, or games. Sunday was reserved for church-going, often a prolonged and formal service of which a hard-hitting theological discourse was the centerpiece. Sitting motionless on hard wooden benches, encased in sober, precise clothing that wasn't comfortably worn-in like weekday apparel—this was Sunday's experience. The Little House stories tell of such a Sunday after church when the endless hours of restricted boyhood activity chafed at Laura's great grandfather so that he stole from the house while his own father inadvertently dozed behind the pages of the big Bible. The boy and his siblings had just the day before finished fashioning a hand-carved sled when the arrival of the

Sabbath rest had interrupted them before they could try the sled out. Just a quiet, trial ride and then they would steal back into the house as though nothing had happened—that's what they hoped for. But as they glided noiselessly down an outside slope, the family pig appeared suddenly in their path, too suddenly to avoid being scooped up and carried speeding down the hill on the front of the sled. Needless to say, the animal's frantic squealing brought father back from his nap and straight to the doorway where the errant Sabbath-breakers were duly apprehended and punished. It made a great story told in retrospect.

Sunday observance was not for all of Christian history such a gloomy and restrictive experience, but it has always been central and it was the first of the religious observances that Christians kept. Sunday was the "Lord's Day" and already in New Testament times the followers of Christ gathered on that first day of the week to break bread. It was, of course, not a day off but a work day because the surrounding culture did not recognize its legitimacy. Nevertheless, it was kept with great joy because it commemorated the Resurrection. In fact, fasting and kneeling were expressly forbidden because of the celebratory quality of the day. Although for Christians the Lord's Day substituted for the Jewish Sabbath, it was not until later, and then gradually, that the idea of having a day of rest consecrated to the service of God became part of church and then civil law.

It was particularly in the English Protestant world that the solemnity of the day and rigorous interpretations of what could be allowed on it in a Christian land abounded. During the seventeenth and eighteenth centuries legislation was enacted, then relaxed, then enforced again that would ensure that the Lord's Day was devoted to works of piety and proper worship. Laura Ingalls Wilder's grandfather was heir to that legacy.

I'm not sure many of us would want to return to a devotional world in which small children are required to remain silent and laughterless for an entire day but the basic impulse behind the centuries of legislation, both before and after the Reformation was, I think, a positive one. The notion of a Sabbath (the word comes from the Hebrew *shabbat,* which means to cease or desist) is derived, of course, from Judaism in whose ritual practice honoring God and refraining from work on the seventh day of the week was obligatory. The prohibition from work not only focused attention on God who, the Hebrew Bible tells us, ceased from the work of creation on the seventh day, it allowed a time for lying fallow, for regeneration. Contemporary Jewish writer Abraham Joshua Heschel describes the Sabbath in this way: "eternity utters the day"—a day in which a sampling of the joy, expansiveness, and harmony of God's own time is enjoyed.

There is something really wonderful about the concept of frequently and rhythmically setting aside time for attention to the dearer things of life and for the deep and cleansing regeneration that we all require. Ancient Hebrew custom not only recognized weekly ceasing and desisting, it also recognized a sabbatical at seven-year intervals when the land was allowed to lie fallow and all debtors and Israelite slaves were freed. Sabbath observance was about starting over and regeneration. It recognized that intervals of rest were required for this to happen.

How impoverished our culture has become! Not simply because church attendance has to compete with a thousand other obligations, including employment, but because we live in a twenty-four-hour-a-day, three-hundred-and-sixty-five-day-a-year world. We have no communal time off. Whatever Sabbath keeping we may do is individually orchestrated. And even if most members of our families do follow something of a regular schedule with weekends off, chances are that at some point or another someone will work the late-night shift at a restaurant or the early-morning shift at a hospital. Families whose professions are ministerial are often the worst. They work most on weekends when everyone else has time off. There is precious little common time for regeneration. How significant a cultural fact this is was brought home to me years ago when a religious studies professor made the observation that during the Russian Revolution of 1917 and during the years in which the Communist Party was in power, the rhythms of work in the Sovient Union were intentionally modified so that there was no common weekly time off. A given worker might begin work on a Monday, labor ten days, and then have several days off while his counterpart might begin work on a Wednesday and follow the same pattern. The result was that there was simply no common time. The Party implemented this schedule to make it impossible for potentially dissident groups to gather or for religious communities to have a day for shared worship. The professor called it the homogenization of time. Religious sensibilities, he added, recognize time's variety and texture, recognize that there are sacred times that require acknowledgment, and that common time is necessary for the storytelling that vitalizes our religious vision. How can we know we are beloved daughters and sons if we cannot tell one another, cannot share the ancient tales that carry that knowledge from generation to generation? If we have no shared experience, how can we have shared lives?

Given the overriding importance our culture places on efficiency and economic productivity, it is unlikely that many of us will be entirely successful in restructuring the world in which we live so that year in and year out we may honor the Sabbath rhythms so necessary for our regeneration. But with hope we can celebrate the Lord's Day in a mindful way on a regular basis. Beyond that, we might look carefully for weekly, monthly, or yearly times of family and individual Sabbath keeping—times of starting over, lying fallow, remitting debts. For my family it is the biannual trek to the Rocky Mountains. It is a tradition we inherited from my husband's family. His father, the superintendent of schools of a midsized Kansas town, could not imagine beginning a new school year without a visit to Estes Park. My husband can still point out the cluster of log cabins where they stayed and pitched horseshoes, and he remembers riding on the Tiny Town train, whose colorful conductor kept a running banter going for his grade-school passengers. We honeymooned in those mountains and managed to get there at least a few times when we lived on one or another of the coasts. Since we have lived on the plains for the past decade, our forays to the Rocky Mountains have been possible every other year (visits to relatives in California occupy us on the in-between years). Our visits are less fueled by the tourists' enthusiasm to see new sights than the thirsty doe's longing for running streams: the sheer beauty of the peaks, the inexhaustible wonder of a late-afternoon thundershower, or the miracle of the fog parting in a shrouded valley to reveal a cascade of water. Simply being at the top of the world is enough. We return again and again as an act of Sabbath keeping that makes us mindful of God's goodness and God's majestic creativity and places the frantic, myopic seriousness of our little lives down on the plains in grand and expansive perspective.

During the remaining months between our mountain Sabbaths, we hunt for other minitimes for renewal. Academic life lends itself nicely to periodic withdrawal. Each semester, the teaching schedule changes and it is often possible to arrange intentional time off. For several years, I made it a point to take a day each month for a silent prayer retreat at a nearby house of renewal. My husband pencils in periodic hikes at a local forest preserve. Others I know, whose employment is more time specific, have other ways of finding Sabbath time: a weekly dinner out alone with a spouse, an evening faith-sharing group, a morning Bible study class shared with other mothers of preschool-aged children. Whatever form it takes, a time of touching down into the deep springs that sustain us and coming up refreshed is necessary. It is very much a part of the cyclic rhythm of ordinary time.

Insistently punctuating the whole of our lives as Christians is, of course, the Sunday rhythm. The Lord's Day. It provides the

basic celebratory structure of the church year. It hollows out the
time in which we become a common people with a common
story, sharing a common meal. It is at the Sunday worship that
we as a people hear the Word proclaimed and preached. It is
where we reenact together the ancient table gestures that have fed
generation after generation of believers. This day that memorializes the Resurrection is our opportunity to return together
weekly to the deep substrata that undergirds our ordinary lives,
where the great and final questions that ache inside us, the con-
founding perplexities of our experience, and our most tender
longings are acknowledged and given voice.

★   ★   ★

During the Sundays of Ordinary Time the church reflects together on the ministry and public life of Jesus during the brief
years before his passion. Each of the three variant portraits drawn
by the authors of the books we know as the Gospels according
to Matthew, Mark, and Luke are considered over a cycle of three
years on the liturgical calendar. Each portrait presents a new face
of Jesus, the carpenter's son. Each portrait is shaped by the perspective of its author and the Christian community within which
it was created.[19]

Following the suggestion of biblical scholar Donald Senior, I
like to think of each of the Gospel portraits as giving us insight
into aspects of Jesus' inner life—his heart—the core of his being
out of which all his actions flow.[20] The Gospel of Matthew gives
us a vivid picture of Jesus as compassionate teacher of God's Word
and interpreter of the Law. According to scripture scholars this
First Gospel emerged from a community of Jewish Christians
whose world was being overturned both by the destruction of
the temple that took place in the wake of the Jewish revolt
against Rome and by the influx of new Gentile Christians into
their community, persons who were unfamiliar with the subtle

points of Jewish history and tradition. Matthew's Jesus is a second Moses, a teacher who interprets Judaism's sacred heritage, the Law. That heritage is seen afresh in the light of God's revelation in the person of Jesus.

To be a disciple in Matthew's world is to be one who participates in the New Israel inaugurated by God's being with us. In this transformed world, all relationships between people have reached the integrity intended by God. The divine law is truly fulfilled. The ancient promises have born fruit. God's people live out the hope to which they are called—and Jesus is the great and compassionate teacher in this effort. To be a disciple is thus to learn well the lessons proffered and to act in accord with what one has learned. So often Matthew's Gospel utilizes the contrasting images of light and darkness, taken from the Hebrew Scriptures, to underscore the advent of the transformed quality of the community that Jesus inaugurates.

During the early weeks of Ordinary Time we begin to read the stories of Jesus' public ministry. Prefacing them are the accounts of the baptism in the Jordan and the temptation in the wilderness; we soon move to the inauguration of Jesus' mission and the calling of his disciples. In Matthew's Gospel, among the first to be called are four fishermen casting their nets on the shores of the sea of Galilee. The Gospel writer sets the event in the context of the ancient prophecies so dear to the people of Israel. Through the prophecy, one sees the motif of light emerging from darkness.

He left Nazareth and made his home in Capernaum by the sea, in the territory of Zebulun and Naphtali, so that what had been spoken through the prophet Isaiah might be fulfilled:

"Land of Zebulun and land of Naphtali,
*   on the road by the sea, across Jordan, Galilee of the Gentiles—*
the people who sit in darkness
have seen a great light,

and for those who sat in the region and shadow of death
  light has dawned."

From that time, Jesus began to proclaim, "Repent, for the kingdom
of heaven has come near."
    As he was walked by the Sea of Galilee, he saw two brothers,
Simon, who is called Peter, and Andrew his brother, casting a net
into the sea—for they were fishermen. And he said to them, "Follow me, and I will make you fish for people." Immediately they left
their nets and followed him. As he went from there, he saw two other
brothers, James son of Zebedee and his brother John, in the boat with
their father Zebedee, mending their nets, and he called them. Immediately they left the boat and their father, and followed him.

(MATTHEW 4:13–22)

Discipleship and call are themes to which we are insistently
invited to attend during the liturgical season of Ordinary Time.
Not only the call of Andrew or Peter, but also our own call.
Through the lens of Matthew's storytelling genius we are invited
to be earnest students, sitting at the feet of a teacher whose
prophetic message is rooted firmly in the sacred past and carries
with it God's own compassionate design for a transformed world.
Our lessons cannot be left in the classroom or the church building or the Bible study class, however. These are not mere academic exercises. They are lessons in being participants in a world
transformed. As soon as Jesus has called these first four Galilean
fishermen, we see him ministering to a great many people
around the Galilean countryside—the sick, the possessed, those
racked with pain of many kinds. As word of his activities spreads,
he ascends a mountain (a significant symbolic gesture, for many
prophets, including Moses, often delivered their messages on
mountains) and speaks to the assembled crowds.

Blessed are the poor in spirit, for theirs is the kingdom of heaven.
Blessed are those who mourn, for they will be comforted.
Blessed are the meek, for they will inherit the earth.
Blessed are those who hunger and thirst for righteousness, for they
*   will be filled.*
Blessed are the merciful, for they will receive mercy.
Blessed are the pure in heart, for they will see God.
Blessed are the peacemakers, for they will be called children of God.
Blessed are those who are persecuted for righteousness' sake, for theirs
*   is the kingdom of heaven.*
Blessed are you when people revile you and persecute you and utter
all kinds of evil against you falsely on my account. Rejoice and be
glad, for your reward is great in heaven, for in the same way they
persecuted the prophets who were before you.

(MATTHEW 5:3-12)

Matthew's "Beatitudes" are among the most cherished of scriptural tests. As Sunday-school children we may memorize them or we may come to know them from familiar musical settings sung in worship. But Matthew's vision of those who inhabit the blessed new world, his kingdom, is anything but sentimental. It is a demanding vision. We are all familiar with the rest of the astonishing and difficult words Jesus utters in his Sermon on the Mount. Go, be reconciled with your brother. If your right hand causes you to sin, cut it off. Do not swear. Turn the other cheek. Love your enemies. Give alms and pray in secret. Do not store up treasures on earth. You cannot serve God and money. Do not worry about tomorrow. Stop judging others. Do to others what you would have them do to you. The gate that leads to life is narrow.

This indeed is the outline of a demanding call. Matthew's Jesus concludes with the admonition, "Everyone then who hears these words of mine and acts on them will be like a wise man who built his house on rock" (Matt 7: 24).

It is, quite frankly, an intimidating vision. Yet some in the Christian community have taken up the challenge of this demanding way that inaugurates the world transformed. In the *Lutheran Book of Worship*, listed among the lesser festivals and commemorations for the month of January are the names of George Fox (d. 1691) and Martin Luther King Jr. (d. 1968).[21] Each is identified as a "renewer of society." How fitting a commemorative title for the seventeenth-century founder of the Society of Friends (Quakers) and the great architect of the American civil rights movement and champion of militant nonviolence. For the lives and philosophies of both of these men witness to their being wise and attentive students of Jesus' Sermon on the Mount.

Fox was something of a wild man as a prophet. Dissenters to the established church in England were many in his day, but Fox's radical critique of both the scriptures and authority of the religious status quo and his tenacious and often shocking forms of protest brought him notoriety. He assumed the immediacy of Christ's teaching available to each person through the presence of the "Inner Light." Thus he refused to recognize the necessity for ordained ministry or consecrated places of worship. For Fox all life was sacramental, each believer a recipient of the living Spirit. What was needed was for true believers to gather together in silent attentiveness, waiting for the Spirit to guide them. Early Quakers called themselves Friends of the Light or Friends of the Truth.

One of Fox's earliest followers was Margaret Fell, who later became his wife. Together they created a religious movement that attempted to put into action the transformed world proclaimed in the Sermon on the Mount. "Do not swear" became a refusal to take oaths or give allegiance to any but God. "Turn the other cheek" became a refusal to participate in military service. The

Matthean Jesus' plaint "I was . . . sick and in prison and you did not visit me" (Matt. 25:43) became a call to comfort those in the forgotten hellholes that were part of the English penal system. Plain speaking, plain dressing, refusing to distinguish among themselves on the basis of wealth, position, gender, class, or status group of any kind, the early Quakers attempted to inaugurate a world quite literally transformed by the gospel.

The founder of the Society of Friends is aptly commemorated as a "renewer of society" because his gospel-inspired vision extended way beyond the purview of personal piety or even church life. It was a kingdom vision of a world utterly transfigured. So too did Martin Luther King Jr. cast an eye focused by gospel teaching on the world around him. Not only did King dedicate, in fact give, his life so that persons of color might rightly be named beloved sons and daughters, he struggled to create the conditions through which what he called the Beloved Community might come into being. His was a kingdom vision. He immersed and trained himself in the philosophy and techniques of nonviolent resistance that Gandhi and others before him had explored. Then Martin Luther King Jr. spearheaded a nonviolent campaign to extend American-guaranteed civil rights to the African-American citizens whose rights had since the founding of this country been systematically denied through segregation. At the core of King's philosophy was the Matthean dictum: Love your enemy. This love was not passivity or simple sentiment—for he advocated strenuous resistance against evil of any kind—but the recognition that through the agapic love of Christ we could be empowered to distinguish between the evil structures and vicious acts that supported racism and the persons enmeshed in that evil and viciousness, both victim and perpetrator. Through self-sacrificing resistance and nonviolent refusal to accept aggression and discrimination, King worked to create a world in which all could be freed—not only those who were the targets of racial hatred but also those who inflicted it. Until all persons were free to recognize their common interests and to see in one another God's beloved children, Martin Luther King Jr. taught that God's kingdom would not arrive.

King, and Fox before him, were indeed Christians who grasped the far-reaching implications of being attentive students of the prophetic teacher's astonishing lesson delivered on the Galilean mountainside so long ago. They were men for whom the Lord's Day, the celebration of the Resurrection, was not simply a pious weekly exercise but a vast and transformative vision of a world in which the promise of the Resurrection was a constant, lived reality. They lived in Sabbath time, the time that tastes of eternity, the time in which the height, depth, length, and breadth of God's love can be felt and known.

An Offering

(Early February)

Here I am, Lord.
Is it I, Lord?
I have heard You
calling in the night.
I will go, Lord,
if You lead me.
I will hold Your
people in my heart.[22]

THE FIRST YEAR I BECAME TRULY AWARE OF THE FEAST OF THE Presentation was 1977. I had taken off a semester from graduate studies in religion to assess my life, to listen to the deeper silences beneath the conflicting voices that made demands for my life. Thus February 2 that year fell during my prolonged stay at a Trappist monastery in northern California. I had been with the community for over a month and by this time was fully immersed in the predictable daily rhythm of prayer. So when I made my way from my hermitage tucked in the folds of the redwood forest to the central monastery compound that morning for the celebration of the morning prayer, I was not anticipating anything new. The air was chill but dry and my breath hung in small clouds in the predawn gloom. Nineteen-seventy-seven was a drought year and the usually lush forest floor was littered with parched, brown underbrush that snapped beneath my feet, breaking the great silence.

Something was different this morning, however. When I arrived, the church was empty. Soon one of the sisters entered and wordlessly beckoned me out of the sanctuary to the side of the chapel. There, in the chill air, the community members had lined themselves up against the outer wall. The row of white linen choir robes stood out starkly against the grey concrete of the church exterior. We were going to process into the church. Each of us held a long white taper whose glinting flame wobbled slightly in the outside air.

I have always responded to the theater of religious processions, the marvelous sense of boundary marking that they delineate in time and space; the way they create arenas for the intimation of mystery, the anticipation of sacred happenings. But I had always encountered formal processions in a larger liturgical context, worship services with gathered congregations or village festivals attended by hundreds of onlookers. There was no one but the few of us there, a community of about a dozen. There were no observers, no cluster of congregants in the pews awaiting our arrival, no festive crowds. We were enacting the ritual for ourselves, in the footsteps of countless generations of other worshipers. Taking up the ancient symbols, recreating the solemn, hallowed gestures, entering the ageless dance.

The light from our candles sent sinewy shadows flickering along the wall as we entered the sanctuary one by one, encircled the empty space, and came to rest in a sheltering oval around the square stone altar poised in the sanctuary's center. The Presentation is one of the church's feasts of light. It is known by a number of titles, such as the Presentation of Christ in the Temple, Candlemas, the Presentation of the Lord, or the Purification of the Blessed Virgin Mary, depending on denomination and century. In the past it was celebrated as part of the Christmas cycle, falling as it does forty days after the feast of the Nativity. So the motif of light, which guides much of the symbolism of that extended season, is evident here too: the prophecies of the Daystar from on high, the star that led the wise men from the East, the light to the Gentiles, the dawn of justice, the brightness of the everlasting Light, the true Light, the Light of the world, light come to dispel the darkness of the world.

On the Feast of the Presentation we celebrate the carrying of the light. We memorialize the offering of Joseph and Mary, who carried their infant child and presented him at the temple. As was the custom in ancient Israel, forty days after the birth of a son a mother was to undergo the ritual purification following childbirth and a firstborn son was to be consecrated to God according to the law.

When the time came for their purification according to the law of Moses, they brought him up to Jerusalem to present him to the Lord (as it is written in the law of the Lord, "Every firstborn male shall be designated as holy to the Lord"), and they offered a sacrifice according to what is stated in the law of the Lord, "a pair of turtledoves or two young pigeons."

Now there was a man in Jerusalem whose name was Simeon; this man was righteous and devout, looking forward to the consolation of Israel, and the Holy Spirit rested on him. It had been revealed to him by the Holy Spirit that he would not see death before he had seen the Lord's Messiah. Guided by the Spirit, Simeon came into the temple; and when the parents brought in the child Jesus, to do for him what was customary under the law, Simon took him in his arms and praised God, saying,

*"Master, now you are dismissing your servant in peace,
   according to your word;
for my eyes have seen your salvation,
which you prepared in the presence of all peoples,
a light for revelation to the Gentiles,
and for glory to your people Israel."*

And the child's father and mother were amazed at what was being said about him. Then Simeon blessed them and said to his mother Mary, "This child is destined for the falling and rising of many in

Israel, and to be a sign that will be opposed so that the inner thoughts of many will be revealed—and a sword will pierce your own soul too."

There was also a prophet, Anna the daughter of Phanuel, of the tribe of Asher. She was of a great age, having lived with her husband seven years her marriage, then as a widow to the age of eighty-four. She never left the temple, but worshiped there with fasting and prayer night and day. At that moment she came, and began to praise God and to speak about the child to all who were looking for the redemption of Jerusalem.

(LUKE 2:22-38)

In 1977 in the drought-dried redwood forests the commemoration was once again enacted, and once again the scripture came alive, not only as a sacred memory but as a present sacred event. Offering, consecration. The dedication of the self to God; these occurred once more.

Carried by the pageant underfolding in the morning liturgy, I bore my wavering flame to that gathered circle. Then we broke and solemnly peeled away, woman after woman, to place our individual candles on the altar, to fasten them firmly in a low-sloped bowl filled with fine-grained, chalk-white sand. We each made our silent, consecrated offering. Perhaps because the ritual had caught me unaware and I had not had conscious time to prepare for the Feast, it was an especially graced moment. For I simply offered myself, wholeheartedly, without the reservations or carefully considered qualifications that I might have had I taken the time to anticipate the event.

Somewhat paradoxically, out of that monastic offering gradually emerged a calling to marriage and motherhood. As I listened in the welcome silence, a silence that I coveted greedily, the response came. Return and face the facts of your life. The silence urged me back to the din of a seemingly uncontemplative existence. Only somehow I was supposed at the same time to hold firmly onto the spirit and presence of contemplative silence to which the monastic enclosure gave such easeful access.

From earliest centuries the Feast of the Presentation has fallen on the second of February so often it falls on a weekday, and my observance of the day over the years since that morning among the redwoods has been only fleeting. But amidst the busy rounds of family and work life, I have repeatedly recalled that surprising, fog-shrouded morning when I placed my flickering taper upon the stone altar in the redwood forest and offered my life.

★   ★   ★

In 1997 the Presentation fell on a Sunday. We had been living in Nebraska for a decade, an eventuality I never could have conceived of twenty years before. Right after Christmas my husband and I had received an invitation from a priest-friend to come to his parish and do a brief presentation on the occasion of an event he sponsored annually—mass and lunch for the couples he had married. We were somewhat hesitant. Although both my husband and I are often engaged doing workshops and writing on various aspects of the Christian life, we have rarely presented together. Once, years before, we made a joint presentation to a church group in a blue-collar Massachusetts parish, and it was a disaster of the first magnitude. Not only are our styles of preparation and presentation utterly and frustratingly different, we had wrongly assessed the needs of our potential audience. The ill-chosen title for our talk, "Christian Parenting in the Real World," had drawn out a crowd of agonized parents of inner-city teens desperate for advice about how to deal with their kids' sexually transmitted diseases and drug and alcohol addictions. We, whose eldest at that time was seven, had planned a cozy little chat about how to savor the joys of nursing a newborn and snuggling around the family fire with cups of hot chocolate.

After that debacle, we never presented as a team again. Many things we do well together, but public presentations, we decided, were not among them. So when the invitation came to drive one wintry Sunday to a farm parish about two hours outside Omaha and speak to a gathering of married couples about marriage, my response was incredulous. The two of us have had a rich life together, but I would never claim I have any real wisdom to share with anyone about the practice of marriage. We have had our complement of mountaintop moments, but we have had as well a full complement of dry times, disappointments, disagreements, and discouragement. About the agony and joys of children I have felt prompted to speak publicly; the inner dynamics of marriage leave me more mute.

But the invitation fell on the eve of the twentieth year of our lives together and something prompted my husband to give a conditional positive response to our friend. Perhaps we could each share for five or ten minutes, reflecting on the lessons we felt we had learned over two decades, then open the floor for discussion. After all, the room would be filled with couples, some of whom would be celebrating thirty- or forty-year anniversaries, who probably had a lot more edifying reflections to offer on their shared lives than we did. I agreed.

When we had said we would speak on the first Sunday of February, I had no inkling what the lectionary readings would be. Our assignment was not linked to the scriptural theme of the day. Or so I thought. But February 2 came and I found myself leaving the house at dawn on an ice-bound Nebraska winter morning to drive with my spouse the distance to the little town of Beemer. I knew by then that it was the Feast of the Presentation and I found myself reflecting on the long-ago morning in the redwood forest when I took up my candle in solemn procession. How marvelously fitting, I thought, marriage and motherhood crept upon me unawares out of an offering I made as I celebrated along with Mary and her husband, Joseph, the presentation of their firstborn in the temple. And here I am, two decades later, being caught unaware once again on that same feast. Asked to be mindful of the commitment I have made, asked to reflect on the small story of my own married life encircled by other stories, both present and past, of that same mysterious vocation of a shared life. All the levels and layers of the stories—the mystery of God working and prompting in unexpected ways— in the holy family, in my family, in the families of these yet unknown women and men of outstate Nebraska who raise cattle, work for farm equipment companies, and can corn for the county fair.

Our priest and friend was an accomplished liturgist who divided his time between pastoring in this tiny, rural parish and administering a sophisticated liturgical program for the archdiocese back in the city. He had brought his skills to bear wherever he went. We pulled up before the small church on the outskirts of the little town, a classic, white-steepled edifice built to hold a congregation of about one hundred. The day was cold and clear, and patches of snow from the previous week's storms glistened on the stubbly brown fields surrounding the church. The chill air was pungent with cow manure. Having underestimated our driving time, we were about five minutes late, so we slipped into the back of the church just as the entrance procession was beginning.

Into the sanctuary filed the dozen or so couples gathered to celebrate their shared lives. They outnumbered the assembled congregation. To the elegant accompaniment of a four voice volunteer choir's rendition of an ancient chant, the couples peeled off two by two before the altar rail and joined the congregation. This was full-blown liturgical solemnity—handbells, incense, precise ritual gesture—articulated in the charming, homey accent of the American plains.

So deliciously incongruous was the mixture of plaid flannel and lace filigree I felt transported to some paradisiacal world where all things disparate become reconciled and made one. The particularities of my own marriage, with its midlife, urban, baby-boomer trajectory, were dissolved into the universal. All of us were participants in the ancient rite. One man. One woman. Every man. Every woman. The timeless, ever-ancient, ever-new mystery of cleaving. Lives overlapped. Hearts entwined. Two become one. One become more than solitary self. An inclining toward the other. The offering of self.

The mass played itself out, as it had countless times before, a choreography exercised into the sinews of grandmothers and great-grandfathers, a dance of millennial duration. This time we danced it on whitewashed floorboards in the spotlight of a winter sun streaming through the windows of a country church. We were blessed and whatever halting, flawed offering we had made to one another over the years was transfigured in the context of what had been offered by these paired dozen men and women, by the generations of couples who had knelt to pray on these wooden kneelers, by all marriages blessed, broken, wounded or healed. All the small candles placed on altars everywhere became a blazing light in the fire of their shared burning.

★   ★   ★

A scripture scholar colleague of mine shakes his head and warns his students about taking the call to discipleship, as outlined in Matthew's Gospel, too casually. The Beatitudes are the virtues of a transformed community. They are not impossible qualities to cultivate, but they are not necessarily the qualities women or men innately possess. Nor are they simply qualities meant for the edification or personal salvation of individuals. They are qualities of character, hard and imperfectly won, meant for the transformation of all. They are qualities of God's kingdom. They are the fulfillment of the Law.

Matthew has us envision Jesus the teacher, like Moses, atop the mountain, instructing the disciples in their prophetic and paradoxical lessons. Poverty of spirit. Mourning. Meekness. The thirst for righteousness. Mercy. Purity of heart. Peacemaking. Blessed are these. For the writer of Matthew's Gospel, the kingdom of God is both "already but not yet," the reign of God is inaugurated in this life and perfected in the end time. Ironically, it is those who know their dependence upon God, who hunger for that reign to become reality, who mourn in Zion for God's presence, who know, in their poverty of spirit, that that presence is a gift and cannot be forced—these will receive the divine blessing.

Immediately after offering this strange and wondrous teaching, Matthew's Jesus announces:

> *You are the light of the world. A city built on a hill cannot be hid. No one after lighting a lamp puts it under a bushel basket, but on the lampstand, and it gives light to all in the house. In the same way, let your light shine before others, so that they may see your good works and give glory to your Father in heaven.*
>
> (MATTHEW 5:14-16)

What does it mean to be light to the world? Certainly, in some sense, it means sharing talents, not shading one's lamp under a bushel-basket, as the imagery of scripture suggests. Around campfires, in Sunday school classes, in prayer groups, Christians sing this affirmation over and over again.

> *This little light of mine*
> *I'm going to let it shine.*
> *This little light of mine*
> *I'm going to let it shine.*
> *This little light of mine*
> *I'm going to let it shine,*
> *Let it shine, let it shine,*
> *let it shine.*[23]

But perhaps Matthew's Jesus suggests something even more radical than that. Perhaps we, as pupils of the new covenant, are invited into a reality that includes the generous sharing of our given talents but goes beyond that to participate in a world utterly transformed. For in this First Gospel Jesus speaks prophetically against the backdrop of the ancient longings of the Jews. When Jesus speaks of light, he echoes the ancient auguries of the Hebrew prophets who cry out on behalf of the poor, the widow, the orphan, and the dispossessed.

> *Is such the fast that I choose,*
> *a day to humble oneself?*
> *Is it to bow down the head like a bulrush,*
> *and lie in sackcloth and ashes?*
> *Will you call this a fast,*
> *a day acceptable to the LORD?*
>
> *Is not this the fast that I choose:*
> *to loose the bonds of injustice,*
> *to undo the thongs of the yoke,*
> *to let the oppressed go free,*
> *and to break every yoke?*
> *Is it not to share your bread with the hungry,*
> *and to bring the homeless poor into your house;*
> *when you see the naked, to cover them,*
> *and not to hide yourself from your own kin?*
> *Then your light shall break forth like the dawn,*
> *and your healing shall spring up quickly;*
> *your vindicator shall go before you,*
> *the glory of the LORD shall be your rear guard.*
> *Then you shall call, and the LORD will answer;*
> *you shall cry for help, and he will say, Here I am.*
> *If you remove the yoke from among you,*
> *the pointing of the finger, the speaking of evil,*

if you offer your food to the hungry
and satisfy the needs of the afflicted,
then your light shall rise in the darkness
and your gloom be like noonday.
Then the LORD will guide you continually,
and satisfy your needs in parched places,
and make your bones strong;
and you shall be like a watered garden,
like a spring of water,
whose waters never fail.

(ISAIAH 58:5-11)

Those who respond to the call issued on the mountaintop will not only develop and share their talents with the community, they will also be the agents in overturning the world as it is now configured. As he inaugurates his ministry, as he begins to call to himself the disciples who will walk with him (Peter, Andrew, James, John), the ancient hopes swelling in the breasts of the covenanted people for millennia burst forth to illuminate the dark world.

Land of Zebulun, land of Naphtali,
on the road by the sea, across the Jordan,
Galilee of the Gentiles—
the people who sat in darkness
have seen a great light,
and for those who sat in the region and shadow of death
light has dawned.

(MATTHEW 4:15-16)

How do we become bearers of light, luminous candles that enlighten the darkened corners of the world? Matthew gives no simple blueprint. But we know it when we see it. We know it in the brilliant lives that spring from Christian soil, lives like that of Harriet Tubman, lifelong member of the African Methodist Episcopal Zion Church, whose heroic exploits as abolitionist and underground railroad conductor were suggested to her in divine dreams and omens. A freeborn daughter of former slaves, Tubman was responsible for the daring escapes of three hundred slaves into freedom during the decades preceding the Civil War. Surely a lover of the light, she is quoted as once saying, "I think there's many a slaveholder'll get to Heaven. They don't know no better. They acts up to the light they have."[24]

The light we have today, at least around the issue of slavery, is surely clearer than it was before the Civil War. But there are many shrouds of darkness that still cover our world, still shackles that enslave us. The prophetic spirit that cries out for the freedom, dignity, and liberation of the human community has been heard in every Christian generation. What is the sound of that cry in our world today? How do each of us, and we as communities of faith, become bearers of the light, new Moses' pressing on toward the Promised Land?

I think we begin first by making an offering of ourselves. The Presentation of Jesus at the Temple was the beginning, even before he was humanly conscious of his long and intimate walk with God. If we would walk this way also, we must be brought to the altar and there have the small lights we bring as daughters and sons blessed.

Good Gifts

(Mid- to Late February)

We plow the fields and scatter
The good seed on the land,
But it is fed and watered
By God's almighty hand.

He sends the snow in winter,
The warmth to swell the grain,
The breezes and the sunshine,
And soft, refreshing rain.

All good gifts around us
Are sent from heaven above
So thank the Lord, O thank the Lord
For all His love.[25]

MY EARLIEST MEMORIES OF RELIGIOUS IMAGERY ARE OF TWO familiar and widely popular paintings that decorated the drawing rooms of a generation of believers. I remember the first as looming above a well-stuffed sofa in the cozy living area thickly lined with throw rugs and lace doilies belonging to our down-the-street neighbors, the Shannons. The painting, which dominated the small room, showed two small cherubic children with their arms clutched about each other, crossing a precarious wooden bridge in a darkened wood while a majestic angel hovered benignly above them, gigantic wings outspread in a gesture of divine protection. The other painting, less compelling perhaps to a child whose imagination was more readily piqued by the drama of a possibly collapsing bridge, was of a stately and serious–looking Jesus, his shoulder–length brown hair brushing the folds of his loose white garment, standing before a cottage door about which twined what looked to my eyes like cascades of ivy. Jesus' arm was outstretched and he was poised, ready to knock on the closed door. Whether the painter ever intended it or not (no doubt the verse "Behold I stand at the door and knock" was the inspiration), this image of that Jesus, poised to knock, is forever linked in my mind with the passage which, as a child, I thought of as the "knocking story."

> *Ask, and it will be given to you; search and you will find; knock and the door will be opened to you. For everyone who asks, receives, and the one who searches, finds; and for everyone who knocks, the door will be opened. Is there anyone among you who, if your child asks for bread, will give a stone? If you then, who are evil, know how to give good gifts to your children, how much more will your Father in heaven give good things to those who ask him!*

(MATTHEW 7:7-11)

Our ordinary lives are filled with gifts, the goodness of which is beyond speaking. And it is the awakening to gift and the cultivation of a sense of grateful wonder that I find compelling as I grow older. The "knocking story" has taken on a different face since as a child I associated it with the brown-curled Jesus poised before the cottage door. I suppose I understood the passage mechanically then. Put your money in the machine, get a prize back. Or, God gives good things to the children who are good.

The passage, of course, yields many meanings. Such is the rich nature of the biblical text and our collective interpretations over the years that the Word cannot be exhausted. It speaks of the power of prayer, of the necessity for a searching heart, of the intimacy we share with God, and so forth.

It has come to mean this to me in the second half of my life.

Despite the unspeakable pain of the world, the violence that we inflict upon one another, the personal and communal tragedies that we endure that cry out to what often seems a silent, unyielding heaven, despite this, the intrinsic goodness of life and the most simple and fundamental realities are sheer gratuitous gifts given to be savored.

In the spring semester of the academic year 1997-98, my husband and I and our two youngest children were involved in a semester abroad program sponsored by the university where we are both employed. The program has a slightly different intent than many like university-sponsored programs. It seeks not only to immerse students in a different culture and provide intensive language practice, but also to expose students to the realities of life in the Third World. Our university's program took us to the Dominican Republic, a lively, Spanish-speaking nation that shares the Caribbean island of Hispaniola with Haiti, the most impoverished nation in the Western Hemisphere. As part of their course of studies, our American students, whom we accompanied and to whom we taught two of their required courses, were placed in various service sites throughout the city of Santiago or in the nearby peasant mountain villages.

One of the service sites was an orphanage for mentally and physically handicapped children, and my husband, our two children and I were assigned to work there Friday of each week. By even the most minimal United States standards, the orphanage was unspeakable. Over forty severely disabled human beings were cramped in a tiny, second floor establishment with only the barest sanitary facilities (one toilet, often not working, one trough with a shower attachment). A small, hands-on staff of poor, minimally paid women did the backbreaking work of trying to feed, handle, and keep clean forty disabled children (many of whom were incontinent) without adequate supplies. (While donations of disposable diapers showed up often for the infants, older children and adolescents were tied in flannel loincloths or simply stripped of soiled clothing when they had dirtied the bed, floor, or chair where they were placed.) There was none of the rudimentary equipment for rehabilitation or treatment beyond basic health care. The lack was not the result of malice or mismanagement but of stark realities in a nation where basic health care, sanitation, and educational opportunities are meager for the rest of the able-bodied population.

It was there, in that tiny place, among the least of the least, that the simplicity and gratuitousness of the good gifts of life came home to me. There was, of course, the recognition that our First World (especially our American) abundance is something unusual in the global community. I could never take paved roads and access to decent medical care for granted again. Nor could I ever be sanguine about our national habits of excessive accumulation and wasteful use of resources. But that was not what most moved and changed me in my half-year sojourn among the abandoned orphaned children in Santiago. It was the utter grace with which those least among us received the simple gifts of life itself. A touch, a gesture of kindness, a consoling word, laughter: these simple realities stood out in stark relief. Each child was a unique individual with special preferences and personality. We, the visitors, had nothing to give but our presence. Nor did the residents have any more. It was enough.

Among the spiritual treasures of our Christian heritage is the tradition of voluntary poverty. At its root is the concept that the excess we carry with us, both physical and spiritual, burdens us and obscures what is essential in life. Voluntary poverty does not advocate destitution (going without the necessities for a humane life) but a radical simplicity of life and spirit that allows what is essential to be revealed once we are freed from excess burdens. Such "poverty" allows us to see and treasure the gift of life itself, the bountifulness of the good earth, the treasure of each other.

The second half of our twentieth century has seen the flowering of what can be called the "spirituality of the ordinary." We are no longer so interested, as were our Christian forbearers, in a spirituality that free-floats above the human condition. Instead of saints as models of perfection, superhuman virtue, or miraculous attainments, we prefer saints who, despite their flaws, seek to live for others; "warty" saints with whose earthiness and struggles we can identify. Similarly, we have come to see the necessity for cherishing our earth. We search for divine traces in the landscapes and ecological system of which we are an intimate part. Nor do we feel that the Christian life is best fully lived (as did some of our predecessors) by leaving home and family behind. Instead, we trace the features of our loved ones on our hearts and find there our true vocation. Family life has fallen within the circumference of the circles of our spiritual seeking.

What might be termed "family spirituality" today has less to do with Christian education in the home, norms of moral behavior, family church attendance, the practice of religious rituals, or the saying of prayers within the home. Family spirituality has more to do with being formed closely into the image and likeness of God through the involuntary asceticism of family life. It has more to do with discovering the astonishment of God dwelling with and among us in our fallible, fragile lives together. For me, it is especially the mystery of becoming and being a parent that has taught me these essential spiritual lessons: that God is indeed with us, even in the unspeakable confusion of it all. And that I am being formed, through the medium of my children, from the inside out, into someone broader, wider, and deeper than I was.

Any parent knows what it means to welcome a child. The entry of new life does not call for a polite if celebrative ritual and then a return to business as usual. Nor does it mean that you just schedule this person into your established routine like an appointment or meeting. You don't make a little space in your day or share a little concern and then wish the infant godspeed. To welcome a child is to accept responsibility for another person twenty-four hours a day, seven days a week, for a good many years. Ultimately, it is to welcome the unfolding mystery of an entire lifetime's joys and pains as your own.

To welcome a child is to give priority to the unpredictability of another life, to tend it in sickness, no matter what you had otherwise planned, to allow your plans and dreams to be altered, even set aside, because of another's need. To welcome a child is to learn to think and speak in response to a different and constantly changing worldview, to be outside of your own frame of reference. It is to learn patience and judgment and be confronted with your own real and heretofore untested limitations. To welcome a child is to recognize the surprising expansiveness of your own capacity to love and to confront the shattering truth of your own violence and self-centeredness.

To welcome a child is to have your heart stretched, made capable of loving in a new and unrepeatable way. To love in this way is quite different from the love elicited by a beloved, a spouse, or a friend. Each of these loves too has its heart-stretching capacity, but they tend more to equality and mutuality, to the alignment of interest and point of view. They involve companionship, partnership, and the convergence of experiences.

A parent's love is different. It opens places in the heart that have never been exposed before. It awakens inexpressible tenderness, an awareness of the extraordinary beauty and terrifying fragility of human life. It calls forth hope, an almost giddy consciousness of the promise of what might be.

To watch each child unfold the mysterious uniqueness of his or her life is to have your deepest longings called forth. One need only be in a roomful of parents as they witness their children's First Communion or sing at the Christmas pageant with the kindergarten class to sense how deeply, how poignantly, the hope flows. Yet to see how, little by little, the wonder of each life is stunted, crippled, or wounded by bitter encounters with the harshness of social realities, by illness and accident, by innate limitations, is to risk the loss of hope. To welcome a child is to have the doors of the heart flung wide open to embrace the fullness of life, both at its sweetest and at its most bitter. To love with the welcoming embrace of a parent stretches to the furthest extent the contours of the heart.[26]

To enter into the mystery of life in family is to enter into the mystery that is God.

★   ★   ★

Recently I ran across an old photo of our eldest daughter, age five, taken in 1983 during a family vacation to Ensenada, on the northern coast of Mexico. She is seated on the floor next to a low coffee table in front of the free-standing Franklin stove that dominated the tiny living room of the borrowed trailer-turned-beach-cottage in which we stayed. The photo shows her bent intently, straight blond hair falling forward over her cheeks, focused on sheets of red and white construction paper scattered about on the table. She is creating valentines for her nursery school chums back home. Doilies, glitter, and pieces of satin ribbon litter the floor around her.

This past year, on the weekend following Valentine's Day, her father, two young siblings, and I met our blond-haired daughter at the airport in Puerto Plata, Dominican Republic. She had come to visit us during her college spring break, enjoy the tropical beaches, and get some sense of the experience we were having as faculty on the Semester Abroad program. In her bags, she informed us, she carried several proof sheets of the photographs she had taken, part of the portfolio she was developing as a student of the visual arts. As she emerged from the customs area, her wavy blond hair, unfurled from the braids she had worn the night before, cascaded over her cheeks.

It is perhaps a platitude, but that February vacation in northern Mexico with its valentine card litter, seemed in the Puerto

Plata airport only a short while before. Yet the small hand that awkwardly cut through the folds of construction paper then, now deftly handles the chemicals to make photographic negatives and draws in charcoal the figures of live models skillfully enough to win a coveted place in the annual college art show.

Our eldest got her blond hair and hazel eyes from my father, the only blue-eyed, tow-haired member of a family of dark-eyed brunettes. She also inherited from him her artistic gifts—the sureness of her unerring eye that used to assess at her grandfather's bidding the aesthetic significance of "negative space." In his retirement, after decades of designing and retailing his original jewelry, my artist father had become a master calligrapher, transforming the Arabic alphabet into elegant and fanciful forms in his sure, capable hand. During our oldest daughter's high school years, that elder hand had faltered, palsied by age and the debilitating effects of chemotherapy. At the time of his death, my father could barely hold pen to paper surely enough to sign his name on a Valentine's Day card for my mother.

If, as a little girl, I could have asked the "knocking Jesus" for anything, I would no doubt have asked for a fairy-tale life—a life full of beauty and contentment. In fact, on the school playground I used to imagine myself the mother of nine perfectly behaved children (two sets of twins and five singles—I can still name them) aged six months to twelve years, gathered happily and peacefully around me, causing no fuss. As I gaze at the "knocking Jesus" now, I ask instead to see with clearer eyes the gift in what I have been given: a family not without the typical struggle, disappointments, pain, and failure that come with being human. Yet a family who ushers me, with stunning concreteness and particularity, into the mystery at the depth of life.

Family life makes me poignantly aware of mysterious passages of time that mark our growth and change. It ushers me into the unutterable paradoxes and questions that reside at the core of ex-

perience. Family life makes me a seeker. It turns me into someone who stands knocking at the door, someone who, having received the good gifts of life itself, turns them over in awe,
wonder, and wordless gratitude.

II.

The Way That Lies Before

(Time after Pentecost)

Now, my friends. . . . Mend your ways; . . . agree with one another; live in peace; and the God of love and peace will be with you. Greet one another with the kiss of peace. All God's people send you greetings.

The grace of the Lord Jesus Christ, and the love of God, and the fellowship of the Holy Spirit, be with you all.

(2 CORINTHIANS 13:11–13, REB)

Three-in-One

(Sunday after Pentecost)

Holy, Holy, Holy! Lord God Almighty
Early in the morning our songs shall rise to thee
Holy, Holy, Holy! Merciful and Mighty.
God in three persons, blessed Trinity.

Holy, Holy, Holy! All the saints adore thee.
Casting down their golden crowns upon the glassy sea.
Cherubim and seraphim, falling down before thee
Perfect in power, love and majesty.

Holy, Holy, Holy! Though the darkness hide thee,
Though the eye made blind by sun thy glory may not see,
Only thou art holy; there is none beside thee,
Perfect in power, in love and purity.

Holy, Holy, Holy! Lord God Almighty!
All thy works shall praise thy name in earth, and sky, and sea;
Holy, Holy, Holy! Merciful and mighty.
God in three persons, blessed Trinity.[27]

EVERY SUNDAY IT WAS THE SAME. AFTER THE OPENING HYMN, when we had processed into the choir loft, silken red robes brushing our ankles, starched white edges of cottas hemmed so that no matter our respective heights they created a straight line to the gaze of the congregation, we paused. A spoken prayer. Then our imposing six-foot-plus director, with all the weight of his vast knowledge of musicology and the solemnity of a man whose life was given over to the creation of sung prayer, pivoted

79

toward the congregation. Black velvet billowed. Stepping slightly forward, he sang out, "Praise God from whom all blessings flow!"

Organ chords swelled.

"Praise Him all creatures here below." We answered with all our might, individual voices meeting in the surge of sound pressing toward us from the sanctuary.
"Praise Him above, ye heavenly host."
Surely the angels were joining us now.
"Praise Father, Son, and Holy Ghost!"[28]

Every Sunday it was the same at Hollywood First Presbyterian High School Choir. We opened our throats and out flowed the praise of the triune God.

★   ★   ★

Diana L. Eck, a scholar of religion at Harvard's Center for the Study of World Religions, has made the observation that the religious traditions of the Western World—Judaism, Christianity, and Islam—are unique among the world's faiths in claiming that truth is singular. The proclamations "There is no God but Allah," "Thou shalt have no gods before me," and "I am the way the truth and the life" are attestations to this way of thinking. Other cultures have conceptualized truth differently. As perspectival, for example. Eck, a practicing United Methodist whose academic expertise is in Sanskirt and Indian studies, makes her observation not to revive the defunct monotheism-polytheism debate nor to argue for the superiority of one fundamental insight over another, but to help her readers engage in the essential task of respectful and truly informed interfaith dialogue required of citizens of the religiously pluralistic twentieth century. Eck's intent is to encourage readers to genuine reflection on the premises of their own faith communities, to come to know, deeply and intelligently, the principals on which they rest. For most practitioners take for granted or are blissfully unaware of the assumptions that underlie their actions and affirmations.

Of the foundational notions upon which the Christian vision of the cosmos turns, the idea of the triune God—the Trinity—is the richest and ultimately most paradoxical. The one God is three-in-one. Father, Son, and Holy Spirit. Creator, Redeemer, Sanctifier. The idea of a Trinity is, in itself, seen from a global vantage point, a distinct way of interpreting monotheism. But seen from within the diversity of Christian denominations, the doctrine of the triune God is that which binds us together. We may quarrel about the proper expression of the names of the trinitarian God, about the relationships between the three, and about our human relationship to each member of the Trinity. But we in the Western church all share the celebration of Trinity Sunday, observed the week after Pentecost. It is this solemnity that inaugurates the second segment of Ordinary Time.

The Trinity is one of those mysteries that many ordinary Christians would just as soon "take on faith." Indeed, over the centuries among theologians and teachers who trouble themselves with the deep subtleties of such issues, trafficking in theories trinitarian has often been an invitation to be censored by fellow Christians. Among others, Arius of Antioch in the fourth century was firmly denounced for his teaching that the second and third "persons" of the Trinity, the Son and Spirit, were "subordinate" to the Father. And poor Peter Abelard in twelfth-century France was hounded from his teaching post by that spiritual luminary Bernard of Clairvaux for attempting to subject the trinitarian mystery to the scrutiny of human philosophical reasoning while Bernard and his less intellectually adventurous contemporaries would fix a prayerfully contemplative eye upon the triune God and let heart, not head, be guide.

Among those whose bold ruminations on the enigma of

three-in-one have gained acceptance with generations of Christians, Augustine of Hippo is foremost.[29] This early fifth-century
North African was an intrepid seeker from the very first. Before
he became a Christian and a bishop and engaged in the theological reflection that would so shape later Christian thought, Augustine was an ardent student of Greek philosophy and a devotee
in a circle of religious adepts exploring Manichaean teachings.
He finally found his spiritual home in the Christian faith. Augustine was emphatic that the Father, Son, and Spirit constituted
a divine unity of the same substance and equality. They were not
three Gods but one. According to him, to call them a "person"
was misleading, for it seemed to separate the Trinity into discreet
entities.

What Augustine did was emphasize that God is relationship.
God is a dynamic reality whose being is not static but interactive.
And he believed very firmly in the biblical concept that human
beings are created in the divine image. Thus, if we are to understand something about the triune God we should look to ourselves. As in the image of God, there must be in human beings a
unity in trinity. On the one hand, the North African bishop discovered this three-in-oneness in the tripartite nature of the soul
with its memory, understanding, and will. But more signifi-
cantly, Augustine found triune unity in the human experience of
love. Love is not static. It implies relationship. And we know love
in its various expressions. Love cannot exist without a lover, a
beloved, and a loving. Within the Trinity itself God is expressed
as lover, beloved, and the activity of loving. Father, Son, and
Spirit. Mutual reciprocal exchange. God is love. All the wonderful, fluid interchange of never-ending desire and delight. So too
do we most clearly resemble God in whose image we are made
when we are united together through our reciprocal love and
when our hearts incline together toward the source and end of
all our loving—the Triune—God.

The profundity of this fifth-century bishop's insight never

ceases to astonish me. There are aspects of Augustine's thought
that I personally wish the centuries had not reified, but his con-
siderations on the Trinity are rich and suggestive. That God is
love we accept on scriptural authority. But what does that state-
ment mean? The centuries elapsing since the scriptures were
recorded have offered us innumerable insights; surely Augustine's
is among the most provocative. God as Love is relationship. God
as Love is lover, beloved, and the love they share. God is the in-
finite source, the finite expression and the dynamic life between
them. Movement. Desire. Delight. Giving. Receiving. Poured
out. Filled to overflowing. A never-ending, restless stream.

★   ★   ★

Among the most revered of icons of the Eastern Orthodox
tradition is the icon of the Holy Trinity. Many of us in the United
States know it through the artistry of the Russian iconographer,
Andrew Rublev, whose rendering of the traditional image has
been often reproduced. Iconographers are not artists in the Western sense, individual interpreters of reality whose technical mas-
tery is used to communicate a singular vision. Rather, Orthodox
iconographers are sacred artisans who, through the employment
of inherited techniques, faithfully reproduce a "window on
heaven." Through the icon, whose form is believed to have been
revealed in an ancient past, the divine archetype—be it Jesus or
the Virgin or a saint or the moment of the Transfiguration or the
Descent into Hades—manifests itself through the medium of
wood, gold leaf, and paint. You do not properly simply look at an
icon. You gaze upon it with contemplative eyes. And gradually,
over years, the icon communicates its eternal message. You come
to know the infinite, ever-unfolding truth incarnated there just
as you would come to know the ever-unfolding truth of a dearly
loved spouse with whom you had lived for many years.

Rublev's icon of the Trinity gives us a visual window into the mystery of three-in-one. We see before us an evocation of a biblical scene, the tables set by Abraham and Sarah under the oaks at Mamre for the three mysterious visitors who reveal God's face to the patriarch and his wife. In the icon, three angels, identical in face and form, are seated at a low table upon which rests a filled chalice. The tender triangulation of figures and wings strikes one first. Then, the gentle regard of each angelic face as it gazes upon its companions. Burnished gold leaf gleams on a mottled field of beiges and ochres from which the periwinkle blues and velvet browns of the angels' flowing garments stand out in relief. The encircling space between the visitors' inclining bodies seems to create a hollow or lap into which the one who prays with this icon may crawl.

Icons are meant to be prayed with. To the patient, loving gaze they will gradually reveal their depths. Henri J. M. Nouwen, one of twentieth-century America's most admired spiritual writers, reflected upon his experience of being in the presence of Rublev's Holy Trinity.

> As we place ourselves in front of the icon in prayer, we come to experience a gentle invitation to participate in the intimate conversation that is taking place among the three divine angels and to join them around the table. The movement from the Father toward the Son and the movement of both Son and Spirit toward the Father become a movement in which the one who prays is lifted up and held secure. . . .

> As I sat for long hours in front of Rublev's Trinity, I noticed how gradually my gaze became a prayer. This silent prayer slowly made my inner restlessness melt away and lifted me up into the circle of love, a circle that could not be broken by the powers of the world. Even as I moved away from the icon and became involved in the many tasks of everyday life, I felt as if I did not have to leave the holy place I had found and could dwell there whatever I did or

wherever I went. I knew that the house of love I had entered has no boundaries and embraces everyone who wants to dwell there.[30]

★   ★   ★

Depending upon the particular year and the calendrical placement of the extended Easter cycle, we often remember the Visitation during the season of Ordinary Time. That celebration falls on the final day of May and commemorates the visit of Mary to her cousin Elizabeth. The two women, one young, one advanced in age, each bears within herself a wondrous secret. The elder, barren for years and now in the comfortable roundness of her second trimester, knows she will finally see the fruition of her marriage to Zachary. The younger, her skirts not yet showing any sign of the miracle growing inside, greets her relative.

> *In those days Mary set out and went with haste to a Judean town in the hill country, where she entered the house of Zechariah and greeted Elizabeth. When Elizabeth heard Mary's greeting, the child leaped in her womb. And Elizabeth was filled with the Holy Spirit and exclaimed with a loud cry, "Blessed are you among women, and blessed is the fruit of your womb. And why has this happened to me, that the mother of my Lord comes to me? For as soon as I heard the sound of your greeting, the child in my womb leaped for joy. And blessed is she who believed that there would be a fulfillment of what was spoken to her by the Lord."*
>
> *And Mary said,*
> *"My soul magnifies the Lord,*
> *and my spirit rejoices in God my Savior,*
> *for he has looked with favor on the lowliness of his servant.*
> *Surely, from now on all generations will call me blessed;*
> *for the Mighty One has done great things for me,*
> *and holy is his name.*
> *His mercy is for those who fear him*

from generation to generation.
He has shown strength with his arm;
he has scattered the proud in the thoughts of their hearts.
He has brought down the powerful from their
thrones,
and lifted up the lowly;
he has filled the hungry with good things,
and sent the rich away empty.
He has helped his servant Israel,
in remembrance of his mercy,
according to his promise he made to our ancestors,
to Abraham and to his descendants forever."
     And Mary remained with her about three months and then re-
turned to her home.

                                        (LUKE 1:39-56)

   My favorite pictorial depiction of the Visitation was rendered
by a friend of mine, an artist member of a religious community
of priests and brothers. It is known as the *Windsock Visitation* and
was created for a small community of nuns of the Order of the
Visitation of Holy Mary whose neighborhood-friendly monastery is situated in a depressed inner-city area of Minneapolis.
The *Windsock Visitation* shows two African-American women,
one slender, one plump, draped in the brilliant colors of contemporary African fabrics. The two seem to have just danced into the
frame of the painting, for their billowing skirts trail out behind
them as they embrace each other, full-mouthed smiles of delight
caressing each other's faces. Where they meet midcomposition,
belly to belly, the fabric swirls of color create two interlocking
spirals, two whirling wombs of line and form that dance together
beneath the cousins' encircled arms. Behind the younger woman
the tails of a red-orange windsock sway and point to a tumbling

inscription "This is the place of our delight and rest: St. Jane de Chantal."

Jane de Chantal was the early seventeenth-century foundress of the religious order to which the contemporary Minneapolis nuns belong. She and her cofounder, Francis de Sales, Bishop of Geneva, chose the image of the Visitation as an appropriate emblem for their foundation. The monastery was designed as a place of contemplative reflection open to women who, because of advanced age, frail health, physical handicaps, or familial responsibilities after widowhood, could not enter the austere and restrictive contemplative communities of the day. The austerities the Visitation women were to practice were primarily interior. A life of physical simplicity, shared prayer, housework, and works of charity performed in the neighborhood: this was the exterior structure that freed them for their true work. Love was to be their calling. Gentle, respectful regard for one another. Patient bearing of each other's infirmities and foibles. Compassionate concern for all with whom they came in contact. Hearts gentled and humble, willing to incarnate the heart of the gentle, humble Jesus who enjoined all to come to Him. The Visitandines were to be Mary with Elizabeth, bearing God within to a neighbor, carrying divine love to one another in the course of a family visit, in the ordinary routine, the small demands of everyday life.[31]

The *Windsock Vistitation* picture was so named because it had become the custom of the Minneapolis Visitandines to hang a colorful windsock on their front porch in the late afternoons, a signal to the neighborhood children that this is now the time that they might gather for reading, crafts, and storytelling. The windsock was a visible signal to the little ones of inner-city Minneapolis of the hospitality that welcomed them as children of God.

★   ★   ★

The biblical story of the Visitation of Mary to her cousin Elizabeth has been infinitely appealing to generations of Christians. And it has yielded rich and varied readings. In seventeenth-century France, the Visitation passage became the inspiration for a community of women with little social status—widows, the handicapped, the frail—who carried divine love to their companions and neighbors in the ordinary acts of gentleness, patience, and mutual regard. Contemporary Latin American Christians have focused upon the astonishing canticle that Mary proclaims. The "Magnificat" is a hymn of promise, of the radical reversal of the world that God's blessing has bestowed. For Latin Americans the "Magnificat" is both a proclamation of the reversal promised in the impending birth of the baby Jesus and the reversal promised to the poor of the world. The "Magnificat" is the liberating hymn sung by those whose lives are stunted by economic and political oppression. It is the cry of the God whose degrading defeat on the cross became the seedbed for a victory that conquered death itself. The "Magnificat" is the triumphant anthem sung by the socially marginalized who know their true identity as daughters and sons of God.

When I gaze upon the *Windsock Visitation* or when I hear the Lucan narrative proclaimed I think of these varied readings, but I think too of the mystery of spiritual friendship. I think of two people joined together through their shared intention that they bear divine life within them and their mutual concern to aid one another in bringing that life to birth.

The public rhetoric of Christianity gives voice to many human relationships—the bond between husband and wife, between parents and children, between pastor and congregant or priest and parishioners. Less attention has been given to the relationship between friends, especially between persons who might be called spiritual friends. If one looks to the past, one will discover two distinct voices in the Christian tradition that speak of friendship to God that the individual undertakes. The first voice is cautious:

human attachments can draw attention away from things divine, "particular friendships" foster intimacy that is antithetical to the nonexclusive agapic love that Christians must cultivate. The second voice is more appreciative: not only is friendship seen as benign and naturally occurring, it is explored, especially as its content is the life in God, as the royal road by way of which one draws closer to one's goal of divine companionship.

Devout Christians have always sought mutual support in their faith. Not only have they worshiped together, they have also formed small communities in order to intentionally grow and encourage one another in that growth. Some groups have self-consciously referred to themselves using the language of friendship: the "Friends of God" was a widespread spiritual movement in the Rhineland and Switzerland in the fourteenth century. The self-designation of the seventeenth century Quakers was "The Society of Friends."

And theorists like the twelfth-century Cistercian monk, Aelred of Rievalux, and the seventeenth-century, cofounder of the Visitation Order, Francis de Sales, wrote about individual friendships as avenues by way of which we go home together to God. Francis wrote to Jane de Chantal of the bond of friendship that brought them together to God in these wonderful words:

> I have never intended for there to be any connection between us that carries any obligation except that of love and true Christian friendship, whose binding force Saint Paul calls "the bond of perfection." And truly it is just that, for it is indissoluble and will not slacken. All other bonds are temporary, even that of vows of obedience which are broken by death and other occurrences. But the bond of love grows in time and takes on new power by enduring. It is exempt from the severance of death whose scythe cuts down everything except love: "Love is as strong as death and more powerful than hell," Solomon says . . . This is our bond, these are our chains which, the more they restrain and press upon us, the more they give us ease and

liberty. Their power is only sweetness, their force only gentleness, nothing is so pliable, nothing so solid as they are. Therefore, consider me intimately linked with you and do not be anxious to understand more about it except that this bond is not contrary to any other bond, whether it be of a vow or of a marriage.[32]

For these thinkers, friendship was a genuine and particular form of love. Neither separate from nor antithetical to the love of God, friendship was a love that was mutual and equal. Unlike other forms of love, for instance the love of a lover that might not be returned or the love between parent and child, which is shared but of differing kind, the love between friends requires both mutuality and equality. If it does not go both ways, there is no friendship. If the partners do not view each other as equals, the exchange cannot be one of genuine friends.

Aelred of Rievaulx and Francis de Sales both explored the love of friends as a medium for spiritual transformation. Clearly, not all friendships have this end or this capacity. Both writers warned against intimate bonds with persons whose main preoccupations were frivolous, self-promoting, or manipulative. The ground of a true spiritual friendship should be each of the partners' abiding love of God and the desire to share that love with another.[33]

To love another as a spiritual friend is not necessarily a pious undertaking, the forming of a "spiritualized," otherworldly bond. Genuine spiritual friendship, like the spiritual life in general, spans the extremes of our lives. Earthly, gritty, fraught with difficulties as well as delight, engaging us at the point our most tender hopes, our most valiant ideals, friendships such as these can be the forge out of which we are hammered into the divine image in which we were originally created.

The mystery of three-in-one reveals that we discover the mystery of relational love at the root of all that is. Lover, beloved, and the love that unites them. Human friendship is part of that mysterious dynamic. It shapes, challenges, draws, and consoles us. Each partner in the dance of mutual desire and delight that is friendship becomes a partner in the hidden dance being danced in the marrow of our bones, the divine dance that exploded into the created universe and that draws all creation back into its fulfillment in the movements of dynamic, never-ending love.

God, whose almighty word
Chaos and darkness heard,
And took their flight:
Hear us, we humbly pray,
And where this gospel-day
Sheds not its glorious ray,
Let there be light!

Savior, you came to give,
Those who in darkness live.
Healing and sign,
Health to the sick in mind,
Sight to the inward blind:
Now to all humankind,
Let there be light!

Spirit of truth and love,
Life-giving, holy dove,
Speed on your flight!
Move on the water's face
Bearing the lamp of grace
And, in earth's darkest place,
Let there be light!

Gracious and holy three,
Glorious Trinity,
Wisdom, love, might:

Boundless as ocean's tide
Rolling in fullest pride
Through the world far and wide,
Let there be light![34]

God's Body

(Second Week after Pentecost)

One bread, one body,
One Lord of all,
One cup of blessing which we bless.

And we, though many,
throughout the earth,
We are one body in this one Lord.[35]

I ONCE TOOK A GRADUATE SEMINAR IN MYSTICISM FROM A renowned scholar of Judaism, a man philosophically trained who was asking questions about the reigning scholarly interpretations of the mystical teachings of the world's great religious traditions. His reading in Christian mysticism was broad and deep. One day, as we were walking across the university campus en route to class he queried me, "Why do people always say that Christianity as a religion takes history seriously? So much of the mystical literature is otherworldly, it soars above the present, postulates a 'cloud of forgetting' between the created world and the devotee, and encourages one to look to heaven or some eschatalogical future." I was fascinated by the observation. Compared to Christianity's forbearer tradition, Judaism, the professor was right. Judaism places historical events in the forefront of consideration. How one lives now, as a covenanted people, is the crux of the tradition. Even Hasidism, the Orthodox Jewish sect, which bases much of its metaphysics on the otherworldly speculations of the Kabbalah, focuses on the redemptive activity of the pious ones, the Hasidim, as they observe the commandments in the here and now with mystical intensity.

After years of thinking about it, my sense is that the mysticism scholar was both right and not right. He was correct to say that Christianity does not, with the exception of the period of history spanning the birth and death of Jesus of Nazareth, put the accent on a narrative of historical events as the locus where God speaks to humankind.

At the same time he was wrong to see Christianity as essentially otherworldly. For Christianity focuses on the body, on matter itself, as the privileged place where the human-divine convergence takes place. It is this particular focus—on that fleshy intersection—that makes the Christian religion what it is. We are fascinated with bodies: the embodied God known to us in the life of Jesus of Nazareth; the church which we see as Christ's own body continuing his mission on earth; the bread and wine we consume reiterating the sacred words, "This is my body, this is my blood," words we variously interpret yet all repeat; the way in which our embodied experience—our senses, our relationships, the desires of our hearts—give us glimpses of God; the created matter of the earth that we have come to think of as God's body. We are fascinated with bodies.

It is precisely at the portal of human embodiment that we encounter divinity. Infinity comes to dwell with us in the small finitude of a woman's womb. And we gain access to the wideness and immensity of God through the embodied particulars of our own lives.

★   ★   ★

Christianity's insistence that we can know something about God's own life by being exquisitely sensitive to our own embodied sense experience is so wonderfully earthy. "Taste and see," the psalmist issues the provocative invitation.

O taste and see that the LORD is good;
* happy are those who take refuge in him.*
O fear the LORD, you his holy ones,
* for those who fear him have no want.*
The young lions suffer want and hunger,
* but those who seek the LORD lack no good thing.*

(PSALM 34: 8-10)

The Psalms, of course, belong to the tradition of Hebrew poetry to which Christians were heir, but the early followers of the new covenant continued and deeply explored the luxuriant images of taste, touch, sight, hearing, and smell that abound in Hebrew sacred literature. It was particularly in Christian monasticism that taste was explored as a medium of spiritual enjoyment. Generations of monastics confirmed that to pray the scriptures was to eat the Word of God, to take it into oneself, to let it become the food that nourishes and gives life.

Thus Gertrude of Helfta, a thirteenth-century Benedictine could pray:

Blessed the eyes that see you, O God, love . . .
Blessed are the ears that hear you, O God, love, Word of life . . .
Blessed the nose that breathes you, O God, love, life's most dulcet
* aroma . . .*
Blessed the mouth that tastes, O God, love, the words of your con-
* solation, sweeter than honey and the honeycomb . . .*
Ah! Let me taste you thus here, my Lord, for you are pleasant that
* there I may for eternity happily and thoroughly enjoy you, O*
* God of my life. Amen*[36]

To feel hunger and to be filled. What more primal embodied experience is there for a human being? Our tradition urges us to reach down into the most instinctive of urges, physical hunger, to discover an equally urgent longing to be filled. The insistent urgency of hunger is likened to the longing for God. God as nourishment. God as the basic and indispensable sustenance of our lives. Our worship services are luxuriant with imagery of hunger and satiety, with the echoes of our impatient entreaties and God's assurance that we will be fed. All four of the Gospels treat us to some variant of the story of the multiplication of the loaves, a story rich in its evocation of the abundant life with which God wishes to feed us.

> *When the crowds found out about it, they followed him; and he welcomed them, and spoke to them about the kingdom of God, and healed those who needed to be cured.*
>
> *The day was drawing to a close, and the twelve came to him and said, "Send the crowd away, so that they may go into the surrounding villages and countryside, to lodge and get provisions; for we are here in a deserted place." But he said to them, "You give them something to eat." They said, "We have no more than five loaves and two fish—unless we are to go and buy food for all these people." For there were about five thousand men. And he said to his disciples, "Make them sit down in groups of about fifty each." They did so and made them all sit down. And taking the five loaves and the two fish, he looked up to heaven, and blessed and broke them, and gave them to the disciples to set before the crowd. And all ate and were filled. What was leftover was gathered up, twelve baskets of broken pieces.*
>
> (LUKE 9:11-17)

Provocative scriptural passages such as this entice us into exploring our own hunger for God. But I have often wondered if one of the particular challenges for contemporary Christians in affluent countries is to pierce beneath our own peculiar ambivalence about food to discover, perhaps for the first time, the real-

ity of hunger and the delight of being filled. For we are ambiva-
lent about food! In the midst of our almost obscene abundance,
we fret and worry, binge and purge, diet and gorge, and obses-
sively count calories, cholesterol, and fat grams. I sometimes
think if it were possible to take almost any person from another
era in history (perhaps with the exception of a few despotic rulers
or wealthy aristocrats whose decadent lifestyles included continual feasting) and transport him or her into a typical modern
American grocery store, you would probably elicit stunned disbelief. Indeed, if you were to transport almost any person from
one of the rural and depressed areas of two-thirds of today's
world population, you would have a similar response. The sheer
volume and variety of food products packaged, canned, crated,
processed, combined, altered, arranged, homogenized, hydro-
genated, distilled—you name it its been done to it—is astounding. Yet, typically as we push our carts up and down the aisle, we
fret. Some of us may wonder how we can make a pound of
ground chuck stretch with the aid of some macaroni product to
feed ten people. More typically, if advertisements are any indica-
tion, we fret about whether we can spread our toast with a product that tastes like butter but has only half the fat grams, or we
worry over the calorie content of desserts already stripped free of
sugar. Alternately, we brood about the bouquet of a wine we
hope to serve to special guests or the precise location from which
our fresh crabmeat has been harvested. In the midst of all this
abundance (or for some of us, scarcity in the midst of abundance), where do we find grounding for a genuine experience of
hunger and being filled?

Despite our cultural ambivalence, at the very center of our
worship as Christians is the imagery of the table, the banquet set
with bread and wine, that recalls the offering of God's own body
given for us, now become the food that continues to give us life.
We Christians have argued fiercely in the past over our under-
standings of the sacred meal. Sadly, our variant viewpoints con-

tinue to divide us. But we all in some manner acknowledge the fittingness of the symbols and incorporate the ritual of eating at God's table into our shared life.

On the Sunday or the Thursday after Trinity Sunday, members of the Roman and Anglican communions observe the solemnity of the Feast of Corpus Christi—the Body (and Blood) of Christ. The feast was added to the calendar in the thirteenth century, during the era when theological specification was being given to the doctrine of the Eucharist and when devotional attention to the Eucharist was at an intense pitch. It was especially women in contemplative communities, those whom we have come to designate as mystics, who contributed to the Christian community the rich and provocative insights they gleaned from their intimate prayer. The mystery of God's body, the flesh and the blood experienced as most essential nourishment, overwhelmed them.

> *O boundless charity!*
> *Just as you gave us yourself,*
> *wholly God and wholly human,*
> *so you left us all of yourself as food*
> *so that while we are pilgrims in this life*
> *we might not collapse in our weariness*
> *but be strengthened by you, heavenly food.*
> *O mercenary people!*
> *And what has your God left you? He has left you himself,*
> *wholly God and wholly human,*
> *hidden under the whiteness of this bread.*
> *O fire of love!*
> *Was it not enough to gift us*
> *with creation in your image and likeness,*
> *and to create us anew to grace in your Son's blood,*
> *without giving us yourself as food,*
> *the whole of divine being,*

the whole of God?
What drove you?
Nothing but your charity,
mad with love as you are![37]

At the root of these wonderfully vivid mystical insights penned by Catherine of Siena is the deep truth that we are nourished most truly by the food that God offers to us. As a woman of the fourteenth century, Catherine experienced herself as quite literally eating God's body. Her insight here is primordial—to ingest the blood and flesh itself, mysterious sources of life, was to take into oneself a power that was not one's own. To eat and drink another was to become that other. These deep intuitions, certainly, have been variously explicated over the centuries in our varying denominations. As a church our interpretations of this divine partaking span the continuum from literal to utterly symbolic. Be that as it may, the central insight is retained in all corners of the Christian world. We are somehow incorporated (the word itself means embodiment) into God. The church becomes the body of Christ.

★   ★   ★

This Christian insistence on the significance of the body, in all the ways that it developed over the centuries, extends to the incarnate body of Jesus. As I have studied the devotional, artistic, musical, and mystical traditions, I have come to appreciate how the church has undertaken what can only be called a collective and cumulative reading of the text of God's physical body. The community has situated itself at the foot of the cross and gazed in wonder, fear, awe, admiration, horror, and adoration at the wounded flesh. That embodied text has spoken to us of the unfathomable mystery of divine love, a love encoded especially in God's heart.

The cumulative reading began in the patristic era as the church fathers commented upon the Crucifixion in allegorical fashion. For them, the wounded side of Christ from which flowed blood and water was an image of the waters of life that pour forth from the church. Just as Eve came forth from the side of Adam, they said, so the church came forth from the side of Christ. The streams from the side are the sacraments, those grace-filled sources of new life. Not only did the wounded side arrest the church fathers' attention, so did the breast. The Johannine depiction of John the beloved disciple leaning on Jesus' breast at the Last Supper became in patristic exegesis the image of the contemplative soul resting near God's heart, intimate with divine wisdom.

As the centuries unfolded, the church's reading of the body became less allegorical and more literal and devotional. Focus moved away from the victorious cosmic Christ to the human Jesus. The medieval world was particularly devoted to Jesus' human experience, empathic with his pain on the cross, and tender toward him as a vulnerable baby in the manger. The mystery of divine embodiment riveted the attention of the medieval Christian world. The wounded body especially drew them. What was the meaning of a love that spilled out through the open wounds to heal a world? So deep was the devotion to the wounds that contemplative artists, musicians, writers and liturgists produced endless prayers, hymns, and sacred images that hinted at the sublime secrets revealed by the torn flesh of the bodied God.

Associated with more than just the emotional or affective life, the heart was the source of a person's life. Thus to know the heart was to know the person. Gazing upon the cross-hung body, the church saw that an opening was prepared that gave access to the divine heart. And they boldly entered, finding in the mysteries there revealed a source of wonder and awe.

O adorable Jesus, I beseech Thee, when my soul leaves my body, to present and offer to Thy Father the merits of Thy sufferings and grief, and of the five Wounds Thou didst receive for me, in order that, through them, I may be delivered from the perils and grievous extremity of my present state, and saved by Thee, Who hast redeemed me with Thy precious Blood. Amen.

Sacred Side of Jesus, pierced with a lance, and opened that I might enter into the Heart of my God; receive and protect me in the hidden sanctuary of Thy love. O my God, I offer Thee the last sighs of my heart in remembrance of the last sigh of the Heart of Jesus dying on the Cross. I desire nothing else than to end my life in Thy love.[38]

Devotional imagery and language of the Sacred Heart had by the dawn of the modern era permeated the prayer of Christendom. Although during and after the Reformation and after visual and liturgical attention to God's heart became associated with Roman Catholicism, many spiritual renewal movements within the Protestant world retained aspects of heart devotion. The hymns and prayers of the Moravian communities of Eastern Europe are lush with images of the healing blood and the broken body. And Methodism, through John Wesley's contacts with the Moravians, imbibes this same heart spirituality.

To what does all this strange and wonderful attentiveness to the fleshy, enfleshed truth of God's heart and body come? To what does it point? My suspicion is that among the many insights it may give us, this devotional tradition teaches us that at the core of created reality pulses a love that is immeasurably wide and unfathomably deep. The infinite ground of being paradoxically encountered in the most intimate infrastructure of a single cell.

On the Friday following the festal observance of the Body and Blood of Christ, the Roman communion celebrates the solemnity of the Sacred Heart of Jesus. This observance, with its distinctive iconography, has not had a great deal of ecumenical resonance, in part because for several centuries the Sacred Heart served periodically as a standard for the Roman Church, or factions within it, when it saw itself as having a monopoly on religious truth. The feast was officially instituted in the eighteenth century, several decades after Margaret Mary Alacoque, an obscure nun in the provincial French convent of Paray-le-Monial, was the recipient of a series of dramatic visions. In those visions Jesus appeared, displaying his bleeding, wounded heart, and asked that his people institute a feast in that heart's honor so that the immensity of the love that had been poured out for humanity might be acknowledged and indifference and ingratitude toward that love be banished.[39] The litanies that date back from the feast's inception speak of the multifold richness of the symbolism of the heart. In them the Heart of Jesus is a furnace of love, a fountain of grace, the exemplar of virtues, the ravisher and paradise of hearts.[40]

★   ★   ★

In the first decades of this century, a French Jesuit priest and paleontologist, Pierre Teilhard de Chardin, brought together in a rich synthesis the mystical insights from the devotional tradition of the Sacred Heart and the scientific insights gained from his disciplined study of the material world. The result was an astonishing vision of a universe at once physical and spiritual evolving through the millennia toward its evolutionary fulfillment. The earth was being transfigured into its potential Christ nature and within the luminous heart of matter beat the heartbeat of God.

> *Christ. His Heart. A Fire: a fire with the power to penetrate all things. . . .*
>
> *It is as if the fact of bringing together and connecting the two poles, tangible and intangible, external and internal, of the world which bears us onward had caused everything to burst into flames and set everything free . . .*

*Let your universal Presence spring forth in a blaze that is at once
Diaphany and Fire.
    O ever-greater Christ!*[41]

Teilhard learned his science well before the explosion of scientific knowledge that has burst upon the second half of the
twentieth century. But his insights presage more recent Christian reflections that have integrated contemporary concern for the
earth into Christian life and worship. In some denominations the
Lord's Day following Trinity Sunday is observed as Environmental Sunday. Fitting indeed is our shared attention to the created
world which, we no longer see as inert matter provided for
human exploitation, nor as subjected plant and animal species
over which we humans have dominion. Rather, we have come
to appreciate ourselves as an integral part of a marvelously deli-
cate and wise organic life system. We exist in a universe whose
chemical intricacies speak of creative wisdom, the immensity of
whose heavens is billions of galaxies deep, and the complexity of
whose subatomic life dwarfs our imaginations. We have come to
see that the universe is indeed, to use contemporary theologian
Sallie McFague's words, the "Body of God."[42]

On a warm, fragrant evening this past summer I stood barefoot with my seventh-grade son on a neighbor's lawn and peered
through the aperture of a handmade astrolabe at the starry apparition of the night sky. We were trying to locate a seasonally
visible heavenly body somewhere near forty-five degrees, and the
unfamiliarity of the perspective startled me. In the urban envi-
ronment, one's upward gaze is more likely to be directed toward
a devotional image above an altar. Daytime city vision is often
bounded by ceilings, rooftops, or skylines and clear night vision
obscured by the omnipresent glare of electric lights. What passes
for intimate contact with the natural world for many Americans
can be discovered in those nature stores cropping up all over in
shopping malls. There, artificially produced forest scents linger

and recorded music of loons crying contrapuntally with the lush melodies of a string ensemble fill the air. In such stores, artfully packaged bits of the natural world are available for commercial consumption.

But sometimes we get a less commercially orchestrated view of the created world, a more intimate glimpse of the awe full power, the startling depth and breadth of the body of God. Last summer, during our biannual family trek to Rocky Mountain National Park, we attempted a new hike. Our final destination was Sky Pond, a crystalline circle of a lake that rests high above tree line on the east side of the park. We are reasonably adventurous hikers, as multigenerational urban dwellers go, but Sky Pond was a bit more of a challenge than many of our outings. This was in part because after a series of scenic climbs—past the thundering cascade of Alberta Falls, up the rocky slopes along Glacier Creek with a view of the Mummy Range, around the edge of the Loch with its timber pines and wading elk—the hike to Sky Pond ascends to the base of Timberline Falls. There the rocky but distinguishable path dissolves as hikers make their way on hands and knees alongside the rock cliff that edges the falls. Spray from the falls slickens the rocks there and makes the ascent treacherous. Cresting the top of Timberline Falls, one finds oneself in the alpine air where only the vestiges of trees still survive. Craggy cliffs marked by occasional cairns take one around the circumference of the Lake of Glass and then up over another ridge to the rock opening that reveals Sky Pond. What had at the beginning been a well-trafficked path had become a wilderness entered by the hardy few. We were at the top of the world and saw only a half dozen other visitors during our entire time at Sky Pond. Despite our guidebook's warnings that the fierce icy winds blowing into the basin often prevented a long visit, our day was miraculously still and warm. On the smooth rock ledges that shored the pond we unpacked our lunches and ate in the hushed stillness. Barren rock cliffs, almost sinister in foreboding as the swift play of cloud shadows darkened them, rose up behind the pond, to be scaled only by the most determined of well-equipped rock climbers. Sky Pond was majestic both in its bare beauty and its fierceness.

We had trekked the previous four hours by playful mountain brooks, under the canopies of lush pines, by scenic vistas of breathtaking vastness, beside inviting fish-filled lake waters, through damp meadowland color splashed with wildflowers, up the sun-soaked sides of friendly mountains, and been led to the austere beauty of this treeless fairyland of a place.

How little we and the other half dozen souls up there were, how vulnerable, how dwarfed by the imperious majesty of the earth. And how good it was to know that; to know the truth of our little lives, to have our hubris exposed, to see through the lie that the earth is ours to dominate and do with as we wish. Step lightly, for she is as fragile as the minute wildflower surviving the winds on the tundra. Step respectfully, for she is as mighty and untamable as the craggy peaks whose gnarled fingers knock at heaven's door. She is the body of God.

Gathered In

(Late June)

Gather us in—the lost and forsaken,
Gather us in—the blind and the lame;
Call to us now, and we shall awaken,
We shall arise at the sound of our name.

. . . Gather us in-the rich and the haughty,
Gather us in—the proud and the strong;
Give us a heart so meek and so lowly,
Give us the courage to enter the song

. . . Gather us in—and hold us forever,
Gather us in—and make us your own;
Gather us in—all peoples together,
Fire of love in our flesh and our bone.[43]

PERHAPS THE MOST UNUSUAL YET MOST TOUCHING TABLE FEL-lowship my husband and I ever attended took place one summer evening in a private home high in the Rocky Mountains just outside of Estes Park. Our hostess, a local peace activist who described herself as a Quaker-Episcopalian, each month made her living room available for a prayer service and ritual sharing of bread and wine to which a variety of persons from the nearby region were invited to come. "You never know who will show up," our hostess told us. That evening, present beside my husband and me and our three children, were a former priest and ex-nun, now married to each other and practicing psychotherapists; a young couple and their children, the husband of whom was a disaffected Catholic whose sole focus of conversation was the organization of counterrally to offset the excessive zeal occasioned by the Pope's impending visit to Denver; and two young women of vague Protestant affiliation who were clearly a couple and who fussed over the dark-haired toddler they had in tow. The child, we learned, was the product of the two women's simultaneous artificial insemination (one took, the other didn't) as well as their shared love and desire to raise a family together.

These were not the marginalized we Christians usually envision when in our minds we consume a supper with Jesus in modern-day dress. We think sentimentally of the sweet, doe-eyed children that smile out at us from advertisements for Third World hunger relief programs, or righteously of the victims of racial injustice, or compassionately of the blind and the lame, citizens challenged by physical disabilities of a variety of kinds. Gathered here was a motley community of people. To some eyes they may have appeared as unworthy outcasts. But they came with hearts opened and with a hunger for God that would shame the average complacent churchgoer. Each knew him- or herself as a cherished disciple gathered into the table of love.

The second segment of Ordinary Time begins with a celebration of two primal Christian insights: that God is relational, and that divine life is embodied and encountered in the flesh of the world. Swiftly, however, our attention is brought back to the Gospel narratives and we launch in earnest upon the path of discipleship as each of the evangelists envisions it.

That discipleship is indeed a journey, and a long and exacting one at that, is implied by all the gospel writers. But it is the Gospel of Luke and its companion book, the Acts of the Apostles, that image for us most graphically the road upon which we travel. Luke's road is long. It stretches from the dawn of salvation history to the end of the world. His genealogy situates Jesus in a history that extends back beyond Abraham, progenitor of the Jews, to Adam, progenitor of the entire human race. And it is broad. All are invited to travel together: Jew and Gentile, poor and rich, woman and man, the broken, alienated, and lost along with those who are whole and who already belong. For Luke, the kingdom extends to the ends of the earth and the church is heir to the Israelite mission to become a light to all nations and a blessing to the world.

Scripture scholars conjecture that Luke was a Gentile Christian writing about the year 90 C.E. for an audience of Gentiles. Possibly some of them were fairly well-to-do, for there is an emphasis in the gospel on summoning the rich and powerful to their responsibility to the poor. In any case, Luke draws a portrait of Jesus for us that highlights his role as the compassionate, prophetic gatherer of God's people. In this great gathering together no one will be left behind. Luke's Jesus reaches out beyond the margins of Israel's own alienation and oppression—he dines with tax collectors, blesses the woman of questionable repute, heals the blind. And extends his embrace to invite those beyond the boundaries of God's chosen—the centurion's slave, the good Samaritan, even Jairus's daughter, who has slipped beyond the boundary of death. The Lucan Jesus is the great reconciler and the proclaimer of the gospel of peace.

Typically, our second foray into Ordinary Time begins with Peter's confession that Jesus is the Messiah, the Anointed One of God. In each of the Gospels this is depicted as the first time anyone acknowledges the scope and extent of Jesus' life and thus becomes at least dimly aware of the nature of discipleship. Although each of the gospel narratives cast this confession in quite different ways, in each the coming passion is predicted. The path of discipleship is not simply a road to glory. It means walking in the way of the one who suffered and was rejected.

One day when he was praying alone in the presence of his disciples, he asked them, "Who do people say I am?" They answered, "Some say John the Baptist, others Elijah, others that one of the old prophets has come back to life." "And you," he said, "who do you say I am?" Peter answered, "God's Messiah." Then he gave them strict orders not to tell this to anyone. And he said, "The Son of Man has to undergo great sufferings, and to be rejected by the elders, chief priests, and doctors of the law, to be put to death and to be raised again on the third day."

And to all he said, "If anyone wishes to be a follower of mine, he must leave self behind; day after day he must take up his cross, and come with me. Whoever cares for his own safety is lost; but if a man will let himself be lost for my sake, that man is safe."

(LUKE 9: 18–24, NEB)

This notion of a suffering messiah was a new thought for those who gathered around Jesus. God's anointed had been anticipated in the covenant community, but that the chosen one would die an ignominious death was a challenging concept. It was one thing to admit that they had aligned themselves with the emerging reality of God's kingdom. It was quite another to let the radical claims of that kingdom direct their paths.

Throughout the centuries Jesus' pointed question to Peter, "Who do you say that I am?" has resonated through the Christian community. In one sense, the response, following Peter's lead, has been basically univocal, "You are the chosen one of God." You are the word that God wishes us to hear, the heart of God shown to us, the God-directed life acted out for us, the teacher God sends to instruct, the beloved child, the image that reflects our true selves back to us.

In another sense, our responses over the centuries have been multivocal. For each age has depicted Jesus differently, has allowed the good news to unfold in the unique peculiarities of time and place, has interpreted discipleship in light of present historical reality. This is, of course, the great challenge of Christianity, or any founded religion for that matter, to attempt with integrity to discern the original insights of the founder and to allow those insights to come alive in each succeeding age. Each language, each culture, each era refracts the gospel in somewhat variant ways. Just as each of the evangelists refracted the story of Jesus through the lens of the community for which he wrote, we come to the story with lenses of our own focused by the context of our lives. Yet we each must ask the same question, both for ourselves and in conversation with those with whom we worship and whom we would call brothers and sisters. "Who do you say that I am?"

Voices from the last two centuries have given answers very much in the spirit of Luke's Gospel. Jesus is the liberator, the one who gathers in the marginalized and oppressed. While Matthew begins his Gospel story with Jesus teaching on the mountaintop and Mark with an exorcism in the synagogue of Capernaum, Luke begins with Jesus preaching in his hometown synagogue of Nazareth. Standing before an astonished congregation, he reads from the Torah scroll the prophetic words of Isaiah, "The spirit of the Lord is upon me, because he has anointed me to bring good news to the poor. He has sent me to proclaim release to the captives and recovery of sight to the blind, to let the oppressed go free, to proclaim the year of the Lord's favor" (Luke 4:18-19). Then he declares that in their very hearing this text has come true.

So many vital expressions of Christianity in the present century have echoed this sentiment. Fresh theologies of liberation abound: Latin American Liberation theology with its preferential option for the poor, North American Feminist theology with its central interpretive principle of the inclusion and flourishing of women, Black and Womanist theology with their cry against racial injustice and marginalization, Asian Liberation theology, which affirms the right to proclaim the good news in a way that respects the cultural integrity of the Eastern world. We have become aware of the diversity of cultures and perspectives and the way in which the political, social, and ecclesial structures we have created exclude or demean many among us. How, we ask, can we call ourselves God's body when oppression, blindness, and enslavement continue in our churches and our world?

In the context of these realizations, many in the twentieth century have answered the question "Who do you say that I am?" in words that echo the words of Inez, a contemporary Puerto Rican woman who lives in the Bronx and works as an advocate for grassroots Hispanic women's groups.

> *God is strength for the* lucha *[struggle], strength to keep going ahead, to encourage . . . something outside of one that comes to me in the darkest and most difficult moments.*
>
> *Look, I see Jesus as a perfect example of lucha, as a perfect example who broke with all the institutions and with everything that people followed. I see him as a person who in difficult moments, I can sit down, read about, reflect on, and it gives me animo [encouragement] to continue. He suffered; he is a person I admire and contemplate . . . Every person has leaders, and I think that he is the principal leader for me because of the life he led, because of how daring he is many times. And sometimes when I am in difficult circumstances, I say, "In similar situations, how would Jesus have acted?" And I use him as an example.*[44]

The contemporary liberation response to the question, "Who do you say that I am," does not negate the ways in which the church variantly responds in the present or has responded to the question in the past. Indeed, we continue to relate to Jesus as the Rabbi, as the turning point in history, as Light of the Gentiles, as King of kings, Cosmic Christ, Son of Man, True Image, the Crucified, the Monk Who Rules the World, Bridegroom of the Soul, Divine and Human Model, the Universal Man, Mirror of the Eternal, Prince of Peace, Teacher of Common Sense, Poet of the Spirit, the Man Who Belongs to the World—identities we have ascribed to him at various points in our cumulative history.[45] The richness of our multiple evocations speaks not only to the incredible complexity of Christian history but also to the depth, breadth, height, and width of the God whose love continues to pour out, flooding our fields, quenching our thirst, and filling to overflowing the little vessels of our lives.

⋆   ⋆   ⋆

While the church calendar makes note of numerous days in which Christian martyrs, confessors, and saints have entered eternal life, little note is taken of days on which earthly births have occurred. The exceptions to this are Christmas, the day on which Jesus' nativity is celebrated, the birth of Mary (on September 8 if you are a Roman Catholic), and the birth of John the Baptist. This latter is observed on June 24 and on it we read from the Lucan narrative the account of the event.

Now the time came for Elizabeth's child to be born, and she gave birth to a son. When her neighbours and relatives heard what great favour the Lord had shown her, they were as delighted as she was. Then on the eighth day they came to circumcise the child; and they were going to name him Zachariah after his father. But his mother spoke up and said, "No! he is to be called John." "But," they said, "there's nobody in your family who has that name." They inquired of his father by signs what he would like him to be called. He asked for a writing-tablet and to the astonishment of all wrote down, "His name is John." Immediately his lips and tongue were freed and he began to speak, praising God. All the neighbors were struck with awe, and everywhere in the uplands of Judea the whole story became common talk. All who heard it were deeply impressed and said, "What will this child become?" For indeed the hand of the Lord is upon him.

(LUKE 1: 57–66, NEB)

John the forerunner, the one who prepares the way, retains a respected place in our cumulative imagination. We envision him as a tiny infant, the much-wanted son of an elderly barren couple, whose birth was from the beginning surrounded by the aura of prophecy and miracle, proclaimed prophet of the Most High by his own father, the one who will prepare the way for the promised coming of a new dawn. We have wanted to see him, as in our paintings of the "holy kinship," as a ruddy toddler playing with his infant cousin Jesus, secure in the domestic comfort of Elizabeth and Mary's care. We have pictured John as a young ascetic, gripped in the zealousness of his prophetic vocation, the locust-eating, camel's-hair-clad wild man crying aloud in the wilderness, "Prepare a way for the Lord!" Surrounded by his crowd of followers, we have imagined him knee deep in the Jordan, urging all to repent and be baptized. We depict him pouring the waters over Jesus' head, demurring, exclaiming that their roles should be reversed, knowing himself as not worthy even to tie the strap of Jesus' sandal. Finally, we call up our final image of this man, John, his severed head upon a platter served up to the delight of Herod's family, a victim of his own moral denunciations.

When I think of John the Baptist it is mostly in his guise as wilderness dweller. I think as well of a friend of mine from graduate school days who shares John's June 24 birthday and whose life speaks of the extraordinariness of the solitary life. My friend's existence is not heroic. Nor is he a fiery prophet. But he witnesses, in this culture of excessive consumption, frenetic activity, and adulation of power and achievement, to a different reality. He has been single for many years by choice and, although he earned a doctorate in ancient Greek religious philosophies (because he loved the beauty of the language and was moved by the wisdom he discovered there), he has not sought permanent employment in the halls of the academy. Rather, he has held a succession of jobs necessitated by the circumstances of time and place. He has been the live-in gardener on a large estate, managed the night computer operations at a bank, been a research associate on a project on South African indigenous religions, served as a translator and tutor of Greek, and been driver and operations manager for a deliver-to-your-door dry-cleaning establishment. Periodically he has lived in Greece, serving as English language tour guide or, most recently, as winter house sitter on the island of Mykanos.

My friend would no doubt laugh if he knew I thought of him when I think of John the Baptist, for his childhood affiliation with things Christian has long since lapsed. But what I value so deeply, and what in my mind connects my Greek-philosophy-loving friend with the honey-and-locust-eating zealot in the desert, is their shared leanness. Not physical leanness, but their leanness of life. There are very few of us in American culture today who can say that little is enough. My friend currently lives in a rented studio apartment furnished with a futon, one chair, a guitar, a computer, one plate, one cup, one bowl, a knife, fork and spoon, two towels, a few clothes, personal toiletries, and a shelf-full of books. The library he once owned has ended up in a South African university collection. The keyboard he once acquired was sold in a transcontinental move. Away from work, he spends most of his time in solitude, playing his guitar or reading a book. Little is enough. The prestige of a respected career, the comforts of material prosperity, the rich tapestry of swarms of acquaintances, colleagues, and buddies. These are not despised, they are simply seen as not necessary. Little is enough.

This leanness, which my friend comes by with a natural grace, speaks to me of the quality of life into which the wild-haired wilderness prophet invites us. "Prepare ye," he heralds. "Make straight the path." Such preparation, as a spiritual discipline, has almost nothing in common with the busy, frenetic preparations with which we fill our days before the Christmas season. Such preparation has to do with emptying, not filling, with making space rather than crowding it, with letting go, not stocking up. Little must be enough. Otherwise, where in our lives is there room for God?

This truth operates on all levels of our lives. It is a mirror for our hearts, a guideline for our actions, and a cautionary tale for us as communities of faith. Luke's version of discipleship invites us to be, with Jesus, gatherers of the inclusive community, compassionate friend to the marginalized, bearers of light to the entire world. I wonder if we can ever embark on such a path if we lack true leanness in our interior and exterior lives.

★   ★   ★

All three of the synoptic Gospel writers emphasize leanness or traveling light as a condition of being sent forth on mission. The movement of the Sunday narratives as Ordinary Time unfolds urges us beyond the initial calling of the disciples to the experience of being sent. Those who are called are called for a purpose. The kingdom of heaven, God's reign, is imminent. Whether we understand that imminence the way the early church did, as the end of history nearing, or whether we understand imminence as the truth that God's healing, redeeming love waits only for our willing personal response, or whether we understand imminence as the present power of the Spirit acting in our world to overthrow structures of oppression, the Gospels are clear. Newness is at hand. And, having been called, we are asked to be a part of ushering that newness in. Jesus enjoins his followers, and by extension us, to travel light, then he sends us forth.

On one of this teaching journeys round the villages he summoned the Twelve and sent them out in pairs on a mission. He gave them authority over unclean spirits, and instructed them to take nothing for the journey beyond a stick: no bread, no pack, no money in their belts. They might wear sandals, but not a second coat. "When you are admitted to a house," he added, "stay there until you leave those parts. At any place where they will not receive you or listen to you, shake the dust off your feet as you leave, as a warning to them."

(MARK 6:7-12, NEB)

This is lean traveling. In Matthew and Luke's versions of the Missioning, the demands are even more stringent: Take no stick, wear no sandals. Without footwear, fleeing from an enemy would be impossible on the rough terrain of the holy land. Without a stick, one would be defenseless. This Jesus who sends his friends, asks much by requiring little.

Interestingly, the requirements for missioning mirror the ancient customs familiar to those entering the sacred precincts of the Jerusalem temple. Perhaps then such a missioning extends the idea of sacred space and becomes a symbolic action sanctifying the entire world. Indeed, the Matthean and Lucan versions stretch Mark's account in significant ways. Matthew looks ahead to the past resurrection experiences of the disciples and hints at the trials and persecutions they might endure.

Look, I send you out like sheep among wolves; be wary as serpents, innocent as doves.

And be on your guard, for men will hand you over to their courts, they will flog you in the synagogues, and you will be brought before governors and kings, for my sake, to testify before them and the heathen.

(MATTHEW 10: 16-18, NEB)

Luke extends Mark's account differently by including two separate missioning narratives: first of the Twelve, symbolic of the gathered tribes of Israel, and second of the Seventy-two, a number his readers would have recognized as representing all the known nations of the earth.[46] The vastness of the task is evident. The gathering is to be from the four corners. It will include Jew and Gentile, rich and poor, the broken, alienated, and lost along with those who are whole. The seriousness of the sending is emphasized. The readiness to travel lean and light underscored.

Day by Day

(Early July)

Day by day,
Dear Lord, of thee three things I pray:
To see thee more clearly,
Love thee more dearly,
Follow thee more nearly,
Day by day. [47]

AN ASSOCIATE BURST INTO MY OFFICE AND PLUNKED HERSELF down into a chair. "I want it to be Lent again!" she declared. (I noted my calendar. It was a Wednesday in Ordinary Time.) "I loved it then! I was so self-contained, so focused! I fasted and did centering prayer daily. I was disciplined! Then Easter came and it gradually dissolved. And now look at me!" She rifled in her satchel. "This describes it perfectly," she grimaced, producing a journal whose crumpled pages were opened to an article cross-hatched with the scribblings of her pen. It read: "The late Walker Percy is reputed to have said that the greatest challenge of our time may be to get through an ordinary Wednesday afternoon."

There is a resonance to the late novelist's words that makes us feel laughter and melancholy at the same time. Although there is a present vogue in certain circles for the "spirituality of the ordinary," it is nonetheless the sheer tedium of daily life that often thwarts our efforts to sense God present with us. There is a real beauty in ordinary life: the tenderness found with small children, the delight discovered in a well-tended garden, the deliciousness of baking bread. But there is much that is dreary as well. And much that saps energy, deadens the spirit, and leads to distraction:

the onerous tasks that must be done, the trying relationships that must be negotiated, the necessity for constant labor. In the grips of these realities how is it possible to cultivate an awareness of God?

★   ★   ★

Eternity envelopes time. What we often perceive as the passage of time—the swift movement of future disappearing into past, the present crowded with preparations for what is to come, and concern about what has been—is a strange illusion. In truth, we have available to us only the present moment. And in that ever-recurring moment, we have the opportunity to see God. Human beings being what we are, tend to miss the opportunity and let it dissolve into regret for what is missed or disbelief about what might be. "When I get my life organized," we say, "I will make time for prayer."

"If I can overcome this or that bad habit or character flaw, I will be ready for sacred things."

"I should be as holy (or as good, or as disciplined or as loving) as my neighbor (sister, pastor, spouse, or whomever, then I'd be close to God."

These and like protestations are understandable but really beside the point. God's being with us is not a prize won by the best shot at the shooting gallery at the county fair. God-with-us is the reality of our lives. Simply being where we are (rather than where we think we ought to be) is what is most necessary. But in that where-we-are, it is helpful if we can open up windows of time on the eternity—God's time—that surrounds us. It is helpful if we can create gateways in space through which we enter into the divine presence

Christians for centuries have done just that. They have structured patterns of living that encourage them to become aware of the all-encompassing divine presence. They have done this by creating sacred spaces: sanctuaries for worship, gardens, grottoes and retreat houses for reflective prayer, campground bonfires for hymn singing, mountaintop crosses, and shrines at the end of pilgrimage routes. All these become spatial doorways through which the sacred reality is entered.

And they have created sacred time. Time too can become translucent. The Christian community has hallowed Sunday as such a day. So too the week's other days have been punctuated with the daily office in which the ancient psalms and primal words of tradition become once again new. As individuals, Christians have long practiced a multitude of forms of private prayer, thus allowing themselves rhythmic access to God either in informal conversation, formal petition and praise, or in deep silence. Spaces constructed that allow a life to become a sacred architecture. Times orchestrated so that life becomes a symphony played by God.

As one surveys the tradition, perhaps the most obvious example of this kind of God-ward patterning of life is discovered in monasticism. For millennia, Christians have gathered together in intentional communities for the purpose of becoming alive and awake to the divine milieu in which they truly life. Of the many types of monasticism, we in the West are most familiar with the Benedictine tradition. The tradition got its name from its founder, Benedict of Nursia, a sixth-century leader of a group of monks who created for his companions a rule of life that became the most popular monastic rule in the Western church. When we observe Benedict's feast day on mid-July, we memorialize not only the exemplary life of the Italian ascetic but also the Rule of Saint Benedict as well.[48]

Benedict described his community as a "School of the Service of the Lord." The education of the brethren in the ways of God was its primary focus. (Benedict also had a sister, Scholastica, who founded a community for women and who followed her brother's Rule.[49]) The Rule was the primary agent of this education. Necessary not simply to order the practical life of the monastery, the Rule was a tool for spiritual transformation as well for it created an architecture of time and space that was conducive to the practice of the presence of God.

The Rule enjoined the observance of poverty, chastity, and obedience, and the practice of stability. Poverty (as an outer observance) meant giving up personal possessions to join in a life of shared goods. Chastity meant commitment to God alone by renouncing marriage and intimate relations with others. Obedience meant embracing the discipline of the Rule as a pathway to service for the Lord. Stability meant staying in one place and committing oneself to a community intent on shared spiritual growth. All of these practices were intended to free the individual and the community as a whole for attention to the deeper life.

Implied in the monastic way was death to the old, false self cultivated in "the world" and rebirth to the new, transfigured life discovered in Christ. To facilitate this transformation, the Rule outlined a patterned life of prayer and work: *ora et labora*. Work was classically manual work: the labors of growing, harvesting, preparing and distributing food, building, cleaning and tending the monastery structures, care of the sick and visitors, the making and mending of clothing, the administration of the community, and so forth. Prayer was both individual and communal. Each day was outlined so that regular periods of inspirational reading and reflection could complement the main occupation of the monk, the common prayer of the recurring daily offices.

It is the sensible balance of work and prayer, together with the humane advice it renders about mutual responsibility and the exercise of leadership that have given Benedict's Rule its staying power over the centuries. It does allow community members to immerse themselves in the truth of God-with-us. The Rule makes windows in time and gateways in space through which one can peer and enter into the divine milieu.

★   ★   ★

Clearly, most of us cannot or will not embrace the monastic life. Nor is it possible or even advisable for those of us who work, raise families, and are very much citizens of "the world" to mimic a monastic routine. But we can attend to the question of a rule of life. What might that mean for each of us? How might we create windows and gateways in our daily lives?

Commitment to prayer is certainly one aspect of a life rule. That commitment can take many forms. We might find the recitation of the daily office meaningful. Or we might promise God a five-minute-at-a-time, twice-a-day conversation. We might be drawn to the contemplative practice of centering prayer offered in a weekly group and daily on our own. Perhaps we find an end of the day examination of consciousness suits us or that the "Jesus Prayer" or a prayer of the heart gives us life. We might keep a spiritual journal. A brief reading of scripture daily or a more focused engagement in lectio divina might be preferable. Perhaps we meet periodically with a prayer group or a spiritual friend or seek the guidance of a spiritual director. Praying the rosary or a prayerful walk might start our day. Listening to, moving to, or singing devotional music might also suffice. Or perhaps we might simply "offer up" the small pains and delights of our day to God as they occur. The forms and disciplines of prayer are many. What is important is that we make one of them a priority in our lives.[50]

Although the concept of spiritual disciplines is making something of a comeback these days, in some circles there is still resistance to the idea of structured religious practices. No doubt this is because too often traditional practices have been seen as ends in themselves, dutiful chores that the obedient perform to feel righteous about themselves. Religious practices have not seemed to address the needs of society or to speak in the language of our contemporary longings. This, I think, is not so much the fault of religious disciplines themselves, as our failure to appropriate them creatively or understand their true intent. Religious disciplines are formative. That is, they form or shape us. If we allow them to do their true work, they can gradually transform our lives.

Recently, I had the opportunity to walk the labyrinth at Grace Cathedral in San Francisco. There are in fact two labyrinths now at the Cathedral, a nine-hundred-pound tapestry one in the nave of the church and one embedded in a cement terrace outside and to the right of the Cathedral's front doors. Both are copies of the labyrinth designed for Chartres Cathedral in France in the early twelfth century. It was originally built to be walked at the end of a pilgrimage to the holy site. There were any number of great churches designated as pilgrimage sites during the Middle Ages for people who could not make the ultimate pilgrimage to Jerusalem. The Chartres labyrinth is not a maze (nor are any of the many other labyrinth designs). It is not designed as a puzzle to be "figured out." There is only one entrance and one path to follow—to the center—and one returns to the entrance by the same path one goes in. It is, however, possible to get "lost" in the labyrinth. Entered meditatively, the narrow path takes you on a seemingly endless succession of twists and turns, sometimes close to the center, sometimes swinging far out on the periphery. The labyrinth becomes a metaphor for life, a prayerful walk in which whatever prayer or concern you bring seems to become illuminated by the walking itself. Done in concert with other prayerful people whom you meet coming and going along the way, the labyrinth becomes a metaphor for our shared journey.

Specialists in the field of ritual studies will tell you that the powerful effect of the labyrinth walk is not only due to the enthusiasm of the walkers. The very activity of concentrated movement of this sort—circular and constantly changing directions—has a distinct effect on the brain. The ritual action reduces the dominance of the left hemisphere (responsible for analysis and linear thinking) and increases the activity of the right (creativity and associative thinking) creating a "bi-hemispheric" action, a state of mental awareness in which multiple perspectives, paradox, and multidimensional insights are possible.

The labyrinth is only one traditional spiritual discipline among many that have been cultivated in Christian circles. Other practices with which we are more familiar may not even claim our attention as disciplines—hymn singing, for example. It is perhaps no accident that at least two of the Christian liturgical calendars memorialize the great musicians and hymn writers of our tradition. Johann Sebastian Bach, George Friedrich Handel, and Charles Wesley are the most familiar names, but there are many others.[51] If the Psalms were (and are) the sung prayer of the monastic tradition, the hymns of our worship books are, without a doubt, the deepest and most enduring prayers of ordinary Christians. You don't have to be a specialist in ritual studies to know how deeply affecting and beloved certain hymns are. Franz Shubert's "Ave Maria" is a staple of Catholic weddings and funerals and Ludwig von Beethoven's "Hymn to Joy" spills out over denominational barriers to unite all singers in joyous praise.

> *Joyful, joyful, we adore thee,*
> *God of glory, Lord of love;*
> *Hearts unfold like flowers before thee,*
> *Opening to the sun above.*
> *Melt the clouds of sin and sadness;*
> *Drive the dark of doubt away;*
> *Giver of immortal gladness,*
> *Fill us with the light of day!*[52]

Ritual specialists will tell us that focused and disciplined practices are utilized in all religious traditions to encourage expanded states of spiritual awareness. Christian hymn singing might well be included in this category. The point here is that discipline is not best understood as routinization or numbing habituation. Disciplines, if consciously embraced and intelligently guided, can be profoundly formative features of any rule of life.

A rule of life can be as unique as the one who keeps it. It may have specific practices at its core or it may focus on broader attitudes or values that we wish to cultivate in order to more clearly image the God in whose image and likeness we were created.

A number of contemporary writers, no monastics themselves, have plumbed the Rule of Saint Benedict for the wisdom it might shed on the art of being fully human. Among them, British author Esther de Waal has explored the Rule as an inspiration and mentor on the journey. One of the themes she culls from the ancient text is the theme of living with others.

Love dictates the rule of St. Benedict. It is the best guide I know to the hard work of living with other people and loving them as they need to be loved. St. Benedict never promises that loving will be easy. He is totally realistic about the demands and difficulties of any healing and fulfilling relationships. Above all, he has no illusions about the tensions in the art of loving, no illusions about the tensions at the heart of love itself. What he has to tell us does not come across in terms of some abstract moral law or code. Nor does he heap sentimental or romantic expectations on love. He gives us instead a description of how loving relationships are to be fostered in a group of people living at close quarters. In other words he tackles the question of loving at the point at which most of us experience it, that is to say, in the day to day encounter with those amongst whom we have to live.

We learn what this involves by being presented with a portrait. There are a number of chapters which give a vivid picture of the abbot at work, a man whose way of loving is an exemplar for all of us, for the abbot is the good shepherd who holds the place of Christ to the brothers in the community. And he has to live out and show that love in circumstances which are only too familiar to all of us. He is a man under pressure. He carries the burden of administration and of decision-making, and above all decisions about the care of people. From this base we can see that loving people as they really need to be loved is not easy.[53]

A rule of life is not necessarily a schedule of tasks and practices to fill our days. Its intent is to focus our awareness on what is essential—God and the persons among and with whom we are called to live into the promised fullness of life. My own days are filled with the ordinary labors of work and family and, while I try to plan time for reflection and worship, alongside exercise, family time, and the nurturing of others, I have never found it feasible or temperamentally comfortable to be as structured about a day or week as others I know. Instead, I have lived into a different kind of practice that permeates my days. Years ago a mentor of mine presented me with a copy of a little book entitled *The Practice of the Presence of God* by Brother Lawrence of the Resurrection. Lawrence was a lay brother who lived in a Paris Carmelite monastery at the end of the seventeenth century. As a lay brother and not a choir monk, his main chores were in the kitchen preparing meals for the community. Reportedly, his "conversion" occurred at the age of eighteen as a result of seeing a dry, leafless tree gaunt against the snow on a midwinter day. This sight, with the knowledge of the change the coming spring would bring, overwhelmed him with a sense of the power and providence of God. This led him eventually to the Carmelite order and to the cultivation of what he called the practice of the presence of God.

Lawrence was consulted by the well-to-do as well as peasants and housewives. His wisdom was as homey as it was deep. Remember. Continuously. Through a constant, simple attentiveness, cultivate an awareness of God dwelling within. He wrote:

[God] requires no great matters of us: a little remembrance of Him from time to time; a little adoration; sometimes to pray for His grace, sometimes to offer Him your sufferings, and sometimes to return Him thanks for the favors He has given you, and still gives you, in the midst of your troubles, and to console yourself with Him the oftenest you can. Lift up your heart to Him, sometimes even at your meals, and when you are in company; the least little remembrance will always be acceptable to Him. You need not cry very loud; He is nearer to us than we are aware of.

It is not necessary for being with God to be always at church. We may make an oratory of our heart wherein to retire from time to time to converse with Him in meekness, humility, and love. Every one is capable of such familiar conversation with God, some more, some less. He knows what we can do. Let us begin, then. Perhaps He expects but one generous resolution on our part. Have courage.

Accustom yourself, then, by degrees thus to worship Him, to beg His grace, to offer Him your heart from time to time in the midst of your business, even every moment, if you can. Do not always scrupulously confine yourself to certain rules, or particular forms of devotion, but act with a general confidence in God, with love and humility.[54]

★   ★   ★

At the core of any rule of life or any practice of God-directed attentiveness must be a resonance of the kingdom that Jesus proclaimed. In other words, any spirituality, even an intensely pious or zealous one, that closes a person in on him- or herself, that breeds arrogance, hostility, or violence, needs close examination. Religious discipline or devotion is not an end in itself. It is the means by which we are transformed, the crucible through which false self yields to true.

The Gospels are brimming with parables of the kingdom, striking sayings that range from pithy proverbs to little metaphors to elaborate allegories, which speak to us of the values and vision of a world in which God reigns. Midway through Ordinary Time we are treated to a succession of kingdom parables that draw marvelous word pictures of that true life to which we are called and on behalf of which we are sent. By Matthew's parable of the sower we are invited to consider ourselves as the soil, fertile or barren, in which the seed of God's kingdom is sown.

That same day Jesus went out of the house and sat beside the sea. Such great crowds gathered around him that he got into a boat and sat there, while the whole crowd stood on the beach. And he told them many things in parables, saying: "Listen! A sower went out to sow. And as he sowed, some seeds fell on the path, and birds came and ate them up. Other seeds fell on rocky ground, where they did not have much soil, and they sprang up quickly, since they had no depth of soil. But when the sun rose, they were scorched; and since they had no root, they withered away. Other seeds fell among thorns, and the thorns grew up and choked them. Other seeds fell on good soil and brought forth grain, some a hundredfold, some sixty, some thirty. Let anyone with ears listen!"

Then the disciples came and asked him, "Why do you speak to them in parables?" He answered, "To you it has been given to know the secrets of the kingdom of heaven, but to them it has not been given. For to those who have, more will be given, and they will have an abundance; but from those who have nothing, even what they have will be taken away. The reason I speak to them in parables is that 'seeing they do not percieve, and hearing they do not listen, nor do they understand.' With them is indeed fufilled the prophecy of Isaiah that says:

*'You will indeed listen, but never understand,
     and you will indeed look, but never perceive.
For this people's heart has grown dull,
     and their ears are hard of hearing,
     and they have shut their eyes;*

so that they might not look with their eyes,
and listen with their ears,
and understand with their heart and turn—
  and I would heal them.'

But blessed are your eyes, for they see, and your ears, for they hear.
Truly I tell you, many prophets and righteous people longed to see
what you see, but did not see it, and to hear what you hear, but did
not hear it.

  Hear then the parable of the sower. When anyone hears the word
of the kingdom and does not understand it, the evil one comes and
snatches away what was sown in the heart; this is what was sown
on the path. As for what was sown on rocky ground, this is the one
who hears the word and immediately receives it with joy; yet such
person has no root, but endures only for a while, and when trouble
or persecution arises on account of the word, that person immediately
falls away. As for what was sown among thorns, this is the one who
hears the word, but the cares of the world and the lure of wealth
choke the word, and it yields nothing. But as for what was sown on
good soil, this is the one who hears the word and understands it, who
indeed bears fruit and yields a hundred in another sixty, and in an-
other thirtyfold."

(MATTHEW 13:1-23)

In the wonderful Lucan parable of the Good Samaritan we
catch a glimpse of God's law of love that confounds our narrow
perceptions of worthiness and unworthiness, purity and impu-
rity.

  Just then a lawyer stood up to test Jesus. "Teacher," he said,
"what must I do to inherit eternal life?" He said to him, "What is
written in the law? What do you read there?" He answered, "You
shall love the Lord your God with all your heart, and with all your

soul, and with all your strength, and with all your mind; and your
neighbor as yourself." And he said to him, "You have given the right
answer; do this and you will live."

But wanting to justify himself, he asked Jesus, "And who is my
neighbor?" Jesus replied, "A man was going down from Jerusalem to
Jericho, and fell into the hands of robbers, who stripped him, beat
him, and went away, leaving him half dead. Now by chance a priest
was going down that road; and when he saw him, he passed by on
the other side. So likewise a Levite, when he came to the place and
saw him, passed by on the other side. But a Samaritan while trav-
eling came near him; and when he saw him, he was moved with
pity. He went to him and bandaged his wounds, having poured oil
and wine on them. Then he put him on his animal, brought him to
an inn, and took care of him. The next day he took out two denarii,
gave them to the innkeeper, and said, 'Take care of him; and when
I come back, I will repay you whatever more you spend.' Which of
these three, do you think, was a neighbor to the man who fell into
the hands of the robbers?" He said, "The one who showed him
mercy." Jesus said to him, "Go and do likewise."

(LUKE 10:25-37)

Each of the parables is a small universe of discourse that continues to unfold over the centuries, challenging us to self-reflection and confronting us with a vision of self and world that is
often topsy-turvy. I like to think about the parables as a form of
spiritual discipline, verbal labyrinth walks, if you will. Or, to use
an analogy from another tradition, Zen koans. The parables are,
on the one hand, informative. They tell us something about
Jesus' teaching. Through them, we learn about Jesus' God. The
parables are also formative. If prayed reflectively, allowed to enter
one's life, allowed to confront one to become living imagery that
frames our communal and individual lives, the parables can
transform. They sensitize us to the radical reversals and the sur-

prising truths of our faith. They can become the guiding images for our rule of life. In the final analysis, whatever rule of life we develop for ourselves, it must be a rule that facilitates our more fully grasping the mystery of God's kingdom and that gradually prepares us to be rich, fertile soil into which the seeds of that kingdom can be sown.

Much Has Been Forgiven

(Late July to Early August)

Make me a channel of your peace.
Where there is hatred, let me bring your love.
Where there is injury, your pardon, Lord,
And where there's doubt, true faith in you.

Make me a channel of your peace.
Where there's despair in life, let me bring hope.
Where there is darkness, only light,
And where there's sadness, ever joy.

Make me a channel of your peace.
It is in pardoning that we are pardoned,
In giving of ourselves that we receive,
And in dying that we're born to eternal life.[55]

IN THE DOMINICAN CONVENT OF SAN MARCO IN FLORENCE, Italy, on one of the many frescoed walls decorated with the exquisite artistry of the monk-painter Fra Angelico, is a visual representation entitled *Noli me tangere*—"Do not touch me." Fra Angelico's graceful Jesus, fresh risen from the grave, pauses lightly upon the leafy vegetation carpeting the garden. He has turned away from the opened door of the tomb that leans against the left border of the fresco and now twists his upper body around and half turns back. Kneeling on the earth before the tomb is Mary Magdalene, her long red hair flowing over her shoulders. She reaches out to touch him, her face conveying all the delicacy and sweetness of the Dominican artist's art. Her eyes and Jesus' meet at a point directly in the painting's center, just in the foreground

of the trunk of one of a sparse grove of trees. The small space between their outstretched hands seems to pulse with energy. "Do
not touch me," he says, but the gentle expression that crosses his
face and the poignantly outstretched longing in his fingertips be-
lies his words. He has loved this woman, and she him. While they
cannot now join hands, the tightly woven fabric of the former life
they have shared binds them inexorably together.

On July 22, the calendars of the Episcopal, Roman, Lutheran,
and Methodist churches note the day reserved for Mary Magdalene. This woman, known first through the scripture, attained
mythical proportions over the course of the Christian centuries.
The biblical text uses her name specifically in several places—as
a follower out of whom Jesus cast "seven devils" and who ministered to him in Galilee (Luke 8:2), as one of the women who
stood at the foot of the cross (Mark 15:40), as one who discovered the empty tomb and received the news of the Resurrection
(Mark 16:1 ff), and as one to whom the risen Christ first appeared
(Matthew 28: 9, John 20:11 ff). It is the account recorded by John
that captures our imagination most poignantly.

*Early on the first day of the week, while it was still dark, Mary
Magdalene came to the tomb and saw that the stone had been removed. So she ran and went to Simon Peter and the other disciple,
the one whom Jesus loved, and said to them, "They have taken the
Lord out of the tomb, and we don't know where they have laid
him."*

*But Mary stood weeping outside the tomb. As she wept, she bent
over to look into the tomb; and saw two angles in white, sitting
where the body of Jesus had been lying, one at the head and the
other at the feet. They said to her, "Woman, why are you weeping?" She said to them, "They have taken away my Lord, and I
do not know where they have laid him." When she said this, she
turned around and saw Jesus standing there, but she did not know
that it was Jesus. Jesus said to her, "Woman, why are you weeping?*

Whom are you looking for?" Supposing him to be the gardner, she said to him, "Sir, if have you have carried him away, tell me where you have laid him, and I will take him away." Jesus said to her, "Mary!" She turned and said to him in Hebrew, "Rabbouni" (which means Teacher). Jesus said to her, "Do not hold on to me, because I have not yet ascended to the Father. But go to my brothers and say to them, 'I am ascending to my Father and your Father, to my God and your God.'" Mary of Magdalene went and announced to the disciples, "I have seen the Lord"; and she told them that he had said these things to her.

(JOHN 20:1-2, 11-18)

It is as favored disciple, a committed follower whose fidelity to her Lord, even during the dark eclipse of his mission, which was the prelude to receiving the good news, that the church chooses to remember Mary of Magdala today. We celebrate her as a re-markable woman, one of many who were part of the boundary-breaking ministry of Jesus both before and after his crucifixion.

Earlier centuries saw her as a more complex figure. Conflat-ing the scriptural passages in which she is identified by name with other passages in which other women are mentioned, Mary Magdalene became the woman with a questionable reputation (Luke 7:37), who anointed Jesus' feet and was forgiven because she loved much, as well as Mary the sister of Martha and Lazarus, friends of Jesus who lived in Bethany (John 12:3). As such she became the archetype of the repentant sinner, the per-son rescued from the dregs of the world's preoccupation with it-self. Centuries of storytellers embellished her legend. She became for monks in the early centuries the living sign of a lost one saved by her immense faith and by the power of Christ's redemptive action. They saw her retreating from a life of sin, perhaps prosti-tution, and embracing the austerities of the ascetic life, the per-fect penitent. They contrasted her grace-filled humility with their own monkish propensity to believe they could earn salvation through the efforts of their own prayer and mortification. And artists like Donatello cast her in bronze as an emaciated ascetic clothed only in her long, matted hair.

Renaissance painters preferred to depict her in her more sensual guise, and they gloried in detailing the gleaming golds of her jewelry and the radiant red locks of her flowing hair. Storytellers also found in Mary of Magdala a zealous missionary who traveled widely after the Resurrection, witnessing to the truth of the good news in climes as far-flung as Ephesus and Aix-en-Provence.

Contemporary biblical scholars have retrieved for us a much less archetypal Magdalene. And feminist interpreters have raised rightful objections against a Magdalene who perpetuates harmful stereotypes of women as essentially weak, sensual, seductive and sinful. It is thus appropriate that we have come to appreciate this early friend and follower as a role model of discipleship, she who was the first to bring the news of the risen Lord to the faint hearted apostles who had deserted him in his darkest hour. Yet there is a place as well for the old penitent figure, although perhaps we ought to rename her and leave Mary of Magdala in peace with her resuscitated reputation.

The biblical story perhaps most closely associated with the woman who is a repentant sinner was Luke's version of the anointing of Jesus in the home of Simon the Pharisee (Luke 7:36-50). This unnamed woman, known only for the immorality of her life, managed to intrude herself on a supper party, fling herself before Jesus and, weeping, wet his feet, kiss and wipe them with her hair and anoint them with myrrh. This raised scandalized protests from Simon. But Jesus castigated his host, comparing the woman's generous, loving welcome with his meager hospitality. Her great love proved that her many sins had been forgiven: for where little has been forgiven, little love is shown.

This woman who loves much and is forgiven much continued

down the centuries to attract us as a numinous image of one of the deepest truths of the Christian life—that love and reconciliation are intimately entwined. Luke's casting of the gospel especially emphasizes reconciliation, the joining together of opposites, the gathering in of the marginalized, and forgiving the enemy. Echoes of the ancient Israelite hopes for a world transfigured where lion and lamb lie down together in the peaceable kingdom led by a little child saturate the Lucan narrative. It speaks to the instinct buried deep in the human heart to stand at the still center point of a life and find acknowledged and redeemed there all the disparate threads of experience. To arrive at that still, peaceful center much must be forgiven. But forgiveness is not synonymous with forgetting nor is it an easy glossing over of wrongs done or injuries received. To forgive and be forgiven. To forgive oneself. To know oneself as forgiven by God. These are some of the most mysterious, elusive and transformative experiences of human life. Forgiveness is a divine blessing. It loosens the chains that bind and hold us bound. These are spiritual and psychological truths that pertain to us as individuals as well as communities.

How many instances can any of us name nations, ethnic groups, or families that have continued for generations to hate, brutalize, and feud with one another because of ancient antagonisms never forgiven? How painful are the chains of unforgiveness that fetter victim and perpetrator alike? A friend of mind who has worked closely with chronically ill patients whose maladies do not yield to ordinary treatment, has reported that at the root of many debilitating illnesses is an unforgiven, unreconciled trauma. A slow, painstaking recovery can in many instances be facilitated by beginning to loosen the grip a failure to forgive has clasped upon a life.

That which is unforgiven holds us captive. We are imprisoned by the hatred and malice we clutch in our hearts. I do not mean to suggest that forgiveness is easy or even that it is a swift process.

No. When wrongs have been committed the last thing one wants, or even should do, is claim that the transgression should be overlooked. The aftermath of betrayal or injury is unavoidably rage, hate, self-blame, flight, and fight. It is a long and painful process to move through the stages of healing that must occur for forgiveness to begin. The injury must be named and claimed as part of you, the pain allowed to work for you, the injurer must rightly be blamed, and power and strength returned to the injured. Then, knowing you have experienced pain and overcome it, forgiveness can come as a free act.[56]

Forgiveness can be the great cleansing action that allows one to begin again. Retribution or restitution is not enough. They serve as payback but they do not allow for the deep scouring that is necessary to truly start anew. The ancient Israelites knew the principle well for they instituted the practice of the Sabbath year. Each seventh year was set aside so that all could begin over again: fields lay follow and all debts were forgiven. This crucial period of rest was seen as necessary for the harmonious functioning of society and the fertility of the land. The earth can be depleted, our societies become imbalanced and unjust. Similarly, as individuals and as families we require a time of absolution so that we might truly begin again and become fertile fields that yield a rich harvest.

The prayer most identified with Christianity, the one taught to us by Jesus himself, incorporates the crucial insight that forgiveness is a key ingredient as we live into the promised kingdom. Matthew's version of the Lord's Prayer is perhaps more familiar to us, but Luke's pares the prayer down to its barest form and allows us to see clearly that the art of forgiveness is at the heart of Christ's teaching.

Now it happened that he was in a certain place praying, and when he had finished one of his disciples said, "Lord, teach us to pray, as

John taught his disciples." He said to them, 'When you pray, this is what to say:

> *Father, may your name be held holy,*
> *your kingdom come,*
> *give us each day our daily bread,*
> *and forgive us our sins,*
> *for we ourselves forgive each one who is in debt to us.*
> *And do not put us to the test.*

(LUKE 11:1-4, NJB)

Christianity is in great part about setting things right—with God, with our neighbors, even with our enemies. Forgiveness is the relational art form that creates the possibility for all things becoming new. Forgiveness is, as it were, the key to the kingdom. But we only hold the keys because God first has forgiven us. Divinity inclines to our flawed humanity and proclaims each year a Sabbath year. God forgives debts. God allows the earth the opportunity to rejuvenate and to be fallow and so that the harvest might be rich.

Although forgiveness is a central theme in the New Testament, strangely it was not a theme much developed in the spiritual tradition until the twentieth century. In this present era, the most bloody and destructive in human history, we have begun to intuit that not only can we not live authentically into the kingdom without practicing forgiveness, as a global community we may not survive unless we learn to do so. The theme crops up over and over again in the form of theories of active nonviolence, attempts to use mediation and diplomacy to solve disputes, creative nonviolent approaches to childrearing, interpersonal communication, and public strategy. Perhaps one of the twentieth centuries most dynamic ecumenical movements is founded on the principle of reconciliation. Southeastern France is home to an interdenominational monastic community known as Taizé. The foundation dates to the forties when its founder, Brother Roger Schutz, a young Anglican, realized the prayer he had been praying in solitude for some years. Taizé grew out of the anguish of war torn Europe and its mission reflects the longing for peace born out of human conflict. Brother Roger believed Christians of all stripes must be united to work together for the final reconciliation of all things. Taizé has had an astounding history. The monastic community is only one aspect, the nucleus of a larger dynamic. For years Brother Roger sent out circular letters and he especially addressed the youth of the world. Taizé has become the fulcrum of mass pilgrimages of young people. At Easter time the bare hillsides surrounding the community buildings—they themselves are rather practical structures designed for utility—are spread with a vast carpet of tents, trailers, temporary shelters, and sleeping bags for all the pilgrims who flock there.

Taizé is most familiar to the outside world through its music. Using simple yet gorgeous musical forms such as the litany or the repeated refrain or the chant, Taizé's chief composer, Jacques Berthier, created a sung prayer that unites all who come to and go from that place. Most of the congregational refrains are in Latin, simple phrases of ancient origin: *Veni Sancte Spiritus* (Come, Holy Spirit), *Adoramus te Christe* (We adore you, O Christ), *Dona nobis pacem* (Grant us peace). Usually the verses are sung in various languages, reflecting the vast number of nationalities, ethnic groups, and religious diversity gathered there. Taizé's monks do not only utter their prayer for reconciliation from the south of France, they also go out and travel the world, two by two, as ambassadors of the message of peace and reconciliation, bringing their music and their deep blessing wherever they go.

Perhaps the young people of today sense more vividly then we, their parents, that the world community cannot continue to foster division and ancient hatreds. Each time I teach a world religions course to my college-aged students I am always struck that they long, as a group, to see an end to ancient conflicts. I usually give them an imaginative assignment when we are studying the Hebrew Scriptures as an example of sacred literature: Rewrite the Ten Commandments if you think they need to be rewritten for today's world. Inevitably they wish God had made tolerance of one another a divine command. It may be argued that tolerance is not enough in our present world, if tolerance simply means letting other people alone. We may need more creative ways to facilitate common discussion. But my students, as they imagine carving a new set of tablets, have the right instinct. They know that they inherit a world in which violence, hatred, and brutality are rampant. They know too that such conditions are often bred by our failures to respect, tolerate, understand and learn to live creatively with one another. They know that the forgiveness of debts has not occurred and that the world screams in anguish because of it.

Would that we could come to see this transformative art as the key to our deepest longings. What would we be willing to change to practice it well?

> The kingdom of Heaven is like treasure hidden in a field which someone has found; he hides it again, goes off in his joy, sells everything he owns and buys the field.
>
> Again, the kingdom of Heaven is like a merchant looking for fine pearls; when he finds one of great value he goes and sells everything he owns and buys it.

(MATTHEW 13:44–46, NJB)

★   ★   ★

Among the icons most prominent in the Eastern Orthodox world is that of the Transfiguration. That branch of Christendom, which views itself as the true, unbroken tradition stemming from the early church, proclaims that through the presence of

Christ the entire cosmos has been divinized and transformed. Thus all creation is potentially a window on heaven. The sacred artistry of the iconographer allows the heavenly archetypes to manifest themselves on earth and us to gaze upon them. The divine liturgy celebrates the gathering of heaven and earth. With the congregation and the saints in heaven present, Christ comes and dwells with us. So too, through prayer and self-discipline we can become deified, transparent bearers of the uncreated light to the world. The truth of this many-layered mystery is enfleshed in the icon of the Transfiguration.

All three of the synoptic Gospels contain accounts of the event. Matthew's version reads this way:

> *Six days later, Jesus took with him Peter and James and his brother John and led them up a high mountain, by themselves. And he was transfigured before them, and his face shone like the sun, and his clothes became dazzling white. Suddenly there appeared to them Moses and Elijah, talking with him. Then Peter said to Jesus, "Lord, it is good for us to be here; if you wish, I will make three dwellings here, one for you, one for Moses, and one for Elijah." While he was still speaking, suddenly a bright cloud overshadowed them, and from the cloud a voice said, "This is my Son, the Beloved, with him I am well pleased; listen to him." When the disciples heard this, they fell to the ground and were overcome by fear. But Jesus came and touched them, saying, "Get up and do not be afraid." And when they looked up, they saw no one except Jesus himself alone.*

> (MATTHEW 17:1–8)

The event is significant in the Gospel narrative as it connects the messiahship of Christ with the testimony of the law and prophets, furnishes a proclamation of his sonship and prefigures his glory. But classic commentaries among the Eastern fathers provide a more mystical orientation to the text. They locate the "fact" of the Transfiguration not in the person of Jesus but in the perception of the gathered disciples. It was they who were changed. Their eyes were opened and they perceived the truth of Jesus' person as he was before them. He, fully human, fully divine, was seen to be radiant with the uncreated light of God. So too, each of us is a vessel who, if cleansed, can in some measure reveal that same light. But our seeing must be transfigured, our perceptions altered. We must learn to see what is truly present—God-with-us.

The Eastern church had made room on its calendar for the Feast of the Transfiguration well before the turn of the first millennium. In the West it was not officially instituted until the fifteenth century. Today it is ecumenically celebrated on August 6.

Of the sermons I have heard preached on the Transfiguration, one of the most telling was delivered at a spirituality conference in Saint Louis a number of years ago. For many of us such conferences, if they are well done, are mountaintop experiences. We delve with other like-minded people into the rich reserves of our tradition. We pray together with grace. We attend to what really matters. We are nurtured by faith sharing and by a vision of human life that inspires. We are bathed in an atmosphere of prayer. We wonder, *why can't life always be like this*? The conference preacher that day made us aware of our feelings, which included the vague dread of going back to the flat and doleful plains of our ordinary lives. On the mountaintop it is all so clear. The vistas are so wide, the perspectives so expansive, the insights so deep. We want to stay where we are. He counseled us, however, that in the biblical narrative the disciples must descend the mountain. They go back, imprinted with what they have seen, but they return nonetheless. For the real work of discipleship has really just begun.

Some people drawn to books, lectures, and workshops on the spiritual life have the impression that such a life is essentially about a cocoonlike state of blissful, stress-free experience. Spirituality seems to them to be about getting centered, being calm, relieving stress, and achieving happiness. Perhaps, in small part, it is. But the spiritual life is first and foremost a life responsive to the prompting of God's Spirit. And the ultimate movement of that Spirit is toward a trans-figured, reconciled world. Some may be prompted to a contempla-tive practice (not to be confused with an idyllic self-fulfillment), others to active mission work, others to community leadership, still others to discipleship in the context of family and work. Despite the fact that the life of prayer (or the contemplative life) and the life of active discipleship have been artificially opposed in the history of the church, there can be no genuine antithesis between the two.

In the past it was often the older "complex" Magdalene figure who was identified with the contemplative life. This was when the Apostle Mary of Magdala was confused with Mary of Bethany re-ferred to in Luke's Gospel. Mary and her brother Lazarus, her sister, Martha, of the town of Bethany were friends of Jesus. One encounter with him while he was visiting their house became the scriptural basis for the opposition of the active and contemplative lives.

> *Now as they went on their way, he entered a certain village, where a woman named Martha welcomed him into her home. She had a sister named Mary, who sat at the Lord's feet and listened to what he was saying. But Martha was distracted by her many tasks; so she came to him and asked, "Lord, do you not care that my sister has left me to do all the work by myself? Tell her then to help me." But the Lord answered her, "Martha, Martha, you are worried and distracted by many things; there is need of only one thing. Mary has chosen the better part, which will not be taken away from her."*
>
> (LUKE 10:38-42)

Mary, symbolic of the one who places herself in intimate proximity to Jesus (in prayer) was frequently held up as superior to Martha who, following the active life, was unduly concerned about unessential things. While it may be true that some persons' lives are primarily active in orientation and others more contemplative, or while it may be true that in certain seasons of our lives we lean toward one orientation or the other, it is not a useful strategy to oppose prayer and work.[57]

The point is not to what one is called. Nor is it the "success" or importance of one's ministry or prayer that is crucial. What is essential is to live deeply into the mystery of God-with-us and to respond generously to the holy presence burning like the eternal flame in the ancient temple at the center of our lives. We may not always be entirely clear about the shape or trajectory of our call. But we reach out, like Mary of Magdala on that first Easter morning, toward Love risen because we cannot do otherwise. Because our love compels us. Because we know how much we have been forgiven, how much we have been loved first.

Is There a Balm?

(Late August)

There is a balm in Gilead,
To make the wounded whole,
There is a balm in Gilead
To heal the sin-sick soul.

Sometimes I feel discouraged,
And think my work's in vain,
But then the Holy Spirit
Revives my soul again.

Don't ever feel discouraged,
For Jesus is your friend,
And if you took for knowledge
He'll ne'er refuse to lend.[58]

HE HATED INACTIVITY FOR HE WAS A BORN SOLDIER, A MAN OF immense passion whose zeal it was to serve the noble Duke of Nájera. But in 1522 Ignatius of Loyola, a Basque aristocrat, found himself confined to bed for several months as he recovered from a leg wound received in battle. The castle where Ignatius convalesced was not noted for its libraries and was far from the lively centers of amusement where he preferred to spend his days. In place of the chivalric romances, which the young military man preferred, reading material in his enforced enclosure was limited to a copy of Ludolph of Saxony's *Life of Christ* and to biographies of the saints. Since these had to suffice, Ignatius read them to pass the time. To his surprise he found them utterly engaging. And, as he was a man possessed of great natural gifts of psychological awareness, he noted that the books had a particular effect on him. Like the chivalrous romances, they excited him and inspired him with notions about an exalted life lived for something greater and more beautiful than himself. Unlike the romances, which left him feeling disappointed and restless once he had put them down, the saints' lives and *Life of Christ* continued to inspire him to heroic heights.

As Ignatius's leg wound healed, his spirit, which until then he would not have considered in need of healing, also began to mend. When he left the castle after his five-month stay he was a man transformed. He hung up his sword, donned the clothes of a beggar, and embarked on a spiritual pilgrimage of the first order traveling first to Manresa, where he fasted and prayed. Unable to reach the Holy Land because of war, he went back to Spain and finally to Paris to embark on a program of study in order "to help souls." From his personal experience of conversion, Ignatius developed his Spiritual Exercises, an intense process of guided prayer based primarily on the life of Christ, that was designed to enable the exertant to identify and align with Christ's unfolding mission and ministry in the world. Ignatius especially focused attention on the dynamics of human desire in this process. By imaginatively entering into scenes like the last judgment or Jesus' passion, the exertant rewove his or her own story into the gospel narrative. In 1534 he and six companions founded the Society of Jesus, a group dedicated to rekindling religious fervor in the church. It gave rise to some of Europe's greatest missionary efforts, educational theories, and institutions.[59]

At the heart of the Christian message is the good news of healing: physical healing, emotional healing, and spiritual healing for each individual and for the world. It is especially Mark's version of the gospel that underscores the essential healing ministry of Jesus and, as a consequence, of the disciples.

Mark's account is thought by scholars to be the oldest of the four gospel narratives. It is certainly the shortest and perhaps the most darkly dramatic of the narratives. The Jesus that Mark presents to us is a healer and exorcist. Unlike Matthew, who has Jesus beginning his public ministry on the mountaintop, Mark has Jesus' ministry begin in the synagogue of Capernaum. As he is teaching, a man possessed by a demon begins to shriek, "What have you to do with us, Jesus of Nazareth?" Jesus in response drives the demon out of the tortured human being, causing the man to convulse and scream until the exorcism has been successful. This is a powerful image and others like it occur over and over in different stories throughout the gospel. In a strange world filled with demons, cries of isolation, humans abused and abandoned, Jesus confronts evil. He drives suffering out and his power heals. These healing stories play a more prominent part in Mark's spare account than they do in other evangelists. They illustrate Mark's conception of redemption: the movement from isolation, powerlessness and dehumanization to restoration, humanization and empowerment. The astonishing restoration of sight and hearing or the renewed capacity to move and walk is recounted over and over again.

On his return journey from Tyrian territory he went by way of Sidon to the Sea of Galilee through the territory of the Ten Towns. They brought him a man who was deaf and had an impediment in his speech, with the request that he would lay his hand on him. He took the man aside, away from the crowd, put his fingers into his ears, spat, and touched his tongue. Then, looking up to heaven, he sighed, and said to him "Ephphatha," which means "Be opened." With that his ears were opened, and at the same time the impediment was removed and he spoke plainly. Jesus forbade them to tell anyone; but the more he forbade them, the more they published it. Their astonishment knew no bounds: "All that he does, he does well," they said: "he even makes the deaf hear and the dumb speak."

(MARK 7:31–38, NEB)

The healing that takes place in Mark is set against a confused, dark back drop. Jesus' closest followers misunderstand him all the time. Not only do they spread the news of the healings when asked directly not to, they consistently seem to get the very idea of discipleship wrong.

> *They now left that district and made a journey through Galilee. Jesus wished it to be kept a secret; for he was teaching his disciples, and telling them, 'The Son of Man is now to be given up into the power of men, and they will kill him, and three days after being killed, he will rise again.' But they did not understand what he said, and were afraid to ask.*
>
> *So they came to Capernaum; and when he was indoors, he asked them, 'What were you arguing about on the way?' They were silent, because on the way they had been discussing who was the greatest. He sat down, called the Twelve, and said to them. 'If anyone wants to be first, he must make himself last of all and servant of all.' Then he took a child, set it in front of them, and put his arm round him. 'Whoever receives one of these children in my name,' he said, 're-ceives me; and whoever receives me, receives not me but the One who sent me.'*
>
> (MARK 9:30-37, NEB)

Most people, I among them, are rather like Mark's distracted disciples, falling asleep when we have been enjoined to stay wakeful, focused on who's going to sit at the right hand (our own "correct" version of faithfulness) instead of on our service, eager to be identified with a successful ministry and to trumpet it about, baffled and blaming when things don't seem to go the way we expect. Whenever I have taught the course in church history to the theology majors in our department, I have come away from the semester stunned by the renewed knowledge of the heroism and vision of the few in each era who really seemed to "get it" and equally stunned at the legacy of the countless Christians who didn't. The infighting, lack of charity, fear, cruelty, suspicion, and ignorance we have exhibited in all eras and denominations exhausts the imagination. All in the name of love.

This is why Mark's Gospel hits close to home. We are all in need of healing. Ironically, we wounded ones are also entrusted with the mission of healing that God offers to the world. Aligned with God's purpose we become wounded healers through whom the miracle of divine healing takes place. This puts enormous responsibility on us to care for ourselves and one another so that our hidden wounds will not become the instruments that inflict injury on others. This is particularly true for people in positions of responsibility within the churches. Our thoughtful and informed ministry to the ministers allows our wounds and weaknesses to become sources of life and wisdom for others. But they must never remain ignored.[60]

Commentators have deduced that the Christian community for whom Mark wrote was a persecuted one and that it bore the sign of suffering. For those believers, aligning with the emerging reign of God was a painful, tumultuous process, much like the frightful convulsions provoked by the exorcism of demons from a possessed body. Mark has Jesus predict his coming passion several times and in each instance the disciples fail to "get it." They are thinking about reward and success or they contradict him. They are a thickheaded, distracted crew blind to the reality that confronts them. Indeed, Mark frames his account of the journey toward Jerusalem with two stories of blindness: the blind man of Bethsaida whose eyes cleared in stages as Jesus lays hands on him (Mark 8:22-26) and blind Bartimaeus (Mark 10:46-52) whose faith that Jesus could cure him caused him to shout out from the roadside and insist that Jesus stop and attend to him. Unlike these men who are physically blind, the disciples are spiritually blind. The latter incapacity is perhaps more serious and yet more consistent with our humanness.

★   ★   ★

Mark is not the only Christian to have articulated a magnificent vision of the gospel-inspired life from within a context of persecution. John Bunyan, a seventeenth-century English Separatist, wrote his literary masterpiece, *The Pilgrim's Progress* in the midst of the conflicts between traditionalists and reforming groups that plagued England in those years.[61] Bunyan was a member of a nonconformist congregation and was recognized as a preacher, thus bringing him into open conflict with the repressive measures instituted during the restoration of the English monarchy. He spent more than a decade imprisoned for his beliefs. Like Ignatius, Bunyan was a perceptive observer of the dynamics of the inner life. Thus he allegorized the map of the spiritual journey, placing his protagonist, Christian, at the center of a drama of intense spiritual war. The pitfalls of Christian life on the road from the City of Destruction to the Celestial City were allegorized in unforgettable ways: the boggy quagmire of the Slough of Despond, the fascinating side road that leads to the delights of Vanity Fair. And there were the virtues that aided Christian, like his encouraging companion, Faithful. What both Ignatius Loyola and John Bunyan gave us were road maps of the journey of inner transformation. The English nonconformist painted a classic allegorical portrait of the process of sanctification as it was understood within his broader Puritan world. Ignatius came from the opposite side of the confessional barriers, but he too left us acute observations about the arts so central to the spiritual life. Discernment is the traditional term for the art of "discerning the spirits." In other words, it is assumed that in the midst of trying to be faithful disciples, we will become aware of many different inner voices, "spirits" the tradition calls them, prompting us to this or that action or attitude. Determining the origins of these varied spirits and identifying the Spirit of God moving in their midst is the crux of the art. Ignatius claimed that the spirits could have various origins: social pressures, personal agendas, the overweening desires of family or friends, the promptings of evil origin and so forth. In our psychological world we might identify some of these voices as our inner wounded child, our inherited "tapes," the collective unconscious, the libido, and so forth.

What is central in the art of discernment is learning to pay attention to the effect of the voices (the way Ignatius did when he read the romance novels as compared to the *Life of Christ*). The Basque developed a cluster of "rules" to help untangle the often conflicting voices based on the experiences of what he called "consolation and desolation." In a sense, both Bunyan's *Pilgrim's Progress* and the Ignatian Spiritual Exercises are modes of inner healing. They lead the pilgrim on a journey of self-exploration that reveals weaknesses and wounds as well as gifts and strengths. What are the voices that continually "tempt" us? What pitfalls and side roads are we teased into taking? Which road leads to the Celestial City? Which voice of the many that command attention is truly the voice of God? These are the thorny questions the art of discernment seeks to plumb.[62]

★   ★   ★

When I think of the healing that is available through the work of wounded healers I think first of the stories my mother used to tell me about Aimee Semple McPherson. Growing up in Los Angeles in the forties and fifties, one was still sure to hear echoes of the tales about this colorful early California evangelist. I'm not sure Aimee would be a candidate for any official calendar of saints although she is honored as the founder of Angelus Temple, the flourishing Church of the Foursquare Gospel near downtown Los Angeles. My memories, fueled by my mother's stories, chiefly place the flamboyant preacher, in flowing white satin garments, astride a mechanical white horse with a bouquet of blood-red roses clutched in her arms. She descends by way of a theatrical flying device from the opened ceiling of Angelus Temple to her beloved people, smiling, waving, and proffering the good news with the toss of a red rose. If she had been alive in Argentina in the forties she could have been Eva Perón. Aimee Semple McPherson was a brilliant promoter, a charismatic charmer, a sincere if eccentric believer, and a genuine healer. She was part of the early Pentecostal movement that swept through Christianity in the early part of this century, a woman caught up in the fire of the Spirit to preach, prophesy, and restore people to wholeness.

Aimee Semple McPherson's extraordinary career spanned continents and denominational boundaries. Among the gifts of the Spirit characteristic of Pentecostalism, she possessed the gifts of tongues, preaching, and healing. When she appeared before enthusiastic crowds always numbering in the thousands, "Sister," as Aimee was known, preached the "double cure" known to the faithful through the lyrics of "Rock of Ages." The "double cure" referred to the salvation of the soul and the healing of the body. Her "illustrated sermons," carried out with appropriate costumes and props, brought her healing message to standing-room-only crowds in the midst of the roaring twenties and the great depression of the thirties.

Dramatic physical healings have been part of the gospel tradition from its inception. All four of the evangelists include them. They were signs to the earliest believers that the reign of God was at hand and the ancient prophesies buried deep in the substrata of Israel's consciousness were about to be fulfilled. Such healings have been a reappearing feature of the Christian landscape since then. Even movements that do not emphasize the dramatic visible gifts of the Spirit, as do Pentecostalism or the charismatic renewal that swept through the mainline churches in the sixties and seventies, have retained a strong sense of the essential healing mission of Christianity and the restorative power of intercessory prayer that makes bodies whole again.

There are other sorts of healing, however, to which the gospel points as well. Restoring the social body is as crucial a task as restoring the physical body. We tend to think of such restitution within the category of justice. And often we separate justice or social outreach from the spiritual life. One is public and communal. The other is private and individual. But they are in truth not separable. God's healing power extends to all sorts of bodies, the physical body, the church body, and the body politic.

A colleague of mine, the pastor of a predominantly African-American congregation, speaks of the particular gift of the Negro spiritual to the wider church community. Spirituals, born as they were out of the intense suffering of an enslaved people, can be viewed as a form of discernment. They begin with a cry and they end with a cry. They invite us to locate the Spirit of God within the present context in which we find ourselves. Our present experience of darkness, of injustice, of pain and desolation becomes the locus of intense listening. Peering into the darkness, uttering the cry, we seek for meaning, we seek to discern what is happening in the darkness itself. And we find, even there, a cry of hope and healing. Hear the anguished lament of Jeremiah—

> How can I bear my sorrow?
>   I am sick at heart.
> Hark, the cry of my people
>   from a distant land:
> 'Is the LORD not in Zion?
>   Is her King no longer there?'
> I am wounded at the sight of my people's wound;
> I go like a mourner, overcome with horror.
> Is there no balm in Gilead,

no physician there?
Why has no new skin grown over their wound?

(JEREMIAH 8:18-19, 20-22, NEB)

The Negro spiritual responds: "There is a balm in Gilead."

The notion of healing in the Christian life is two-pronged and paradoxical. On the one hand, the newness into which we are called promises the restoration of all that is wounded or broken. On the other hand, the newness of God's reign is not yet fully with us. We live in the consciousness of "already but not yet." And we must learn to live creatively in the tension of the time between, both filled with hope and the expectation of healing yet wrestling with that which will not yield to treatment. We come with our blindness, with our wounds, to become part of the healing begun by God.

Lifted Up

(Mid-September)

Lift high the cross
the love of Christ proclaim
'Till all the world adore
His sacred name.
Come, Christians follow
where the master trod,
our King victorious,
Christ, the Son of God! [63]

PERHAPS WE READ *LES MISÉRABLES* IN HIGH SCHOOL OR SAW THE more recent operatic version of Victor Hugo's classic story. At the center of this novel lies the question—What is the nature of God? Jean Valjean, a convicted thief brutalized by the punitive justice system of the French empire, experiences the transformative power of grace when he is forgiven for stealing silver from a compassionate bishop who had given him lodging for the night. Valjean seizes upon the graced moment to begin a new life. That life is not only prosperous but also marked by acts of mercy. Yet he is relentlessly pursued by Javert, an upright official of the regime who is convinced both of the impossibility of Valjean's conversion and of the absolute, unbending justice of God. Throughout *Les Misérables*, which is also a plea on behalf of the poor, Jean Valjean witnesses, much to Javert's consternation and disbelief, to the power of the love that has set him free. What is the true nature of God? Rigid justice? Or a breathtaking mercy that transforms the world? Hugo gives his reader no doubt as to his answer to the question.

Teachers of literature and critics of film will tell you that the imagination of the Western literary world is saturated with the symbolism that derives from the Christian religion. The basic narrative line of the Christian story of fall and redemption, such central Christian concerns as sin, guilt, and conversion, the figure of the suffering servant, the hero who seemingly fails only to be lifted up, these are enduring themes and seminal structures to which Western writers have long turned as they have sought to explore the experience of being human.

At the center of these themes and structures is the symbol of the cross. The stark sign created by the overlay of horizontal and vertical wooden beams. The cross. The mysterious axis upon which heaven cleaves to earth and earth to heaven. The alchemical tree upon which time becomes eternity, and the transmutation of evil into good occurs. The cross.

For centuries Christians have gazed in astonishment at that stark symbol. Indeed, when considered in the context of the other great religions of the globe, Christianity is unique in its preoccupation with the mystery that an instrument of death and torture could be the instrument through which new life and divine grace is forged. The cross is a paradox. And paradox is at the heart of the Christian insight. Life from death. Eternity intermingled with time. Fully human, fully divine. Three in one. Saints but still sinners. Sinners yet saints. Already but not yet. To live in the taut tension of these truths is to live the Christian life. Contemporary spiritual writer Parker J. Palmer captures this tension wonderfully.

> *The cross calls us to recognize that the heart of human experience is neither consistency nor chaos, but contradiction. In our century we have been beguiled by the claim of consistency, by the theory that history in moving toward the resolution of all problems, by the false hope that comes from groundless optimism that all works together for good. And then, when this claim has been discredited by tragic events, we*

have been assaulted by theories of chaos, by prophets of despair who
claim that everything can be reduced to the random play of forces be-
yond all control, of events which lack inherent meaning.

But the cross symbolizes that beyond naive hope and beyond
meaningless despair lies a structure of dynamic contradictions in
which our lives are caught.[64]

Christian thinkers and pray-ers, like Jacob wrestling with his
angel, have wrestled with that paradoxical sign. Palmer views it
against the prevailing philosophies of science and technology that
the modern world has produced. Others have expressed the paradox in the idiom of their own cultures and times.

A number of years ago, on my birthday, my husband and
children presented me with a lovely gift. It was a simple
wooden cross, approximately twenty inches high, fashioned by
an artist in El Salvador whose work came to me by way of "La
Semilla de Dios," a cooperative association that promotes and
distributes handcrafts from the Third World to the First World.
The surface is decorated with bright enamel-like paint in the
vivid, bold style typical of Central American popular crafts. The
images on the cross shape are, paradoxically, from another part
of the Christian story than the ones we ordinarily associate
with the cross. At the base of the vertical beam is a large smiling angel, her robe criss crossed with geometric designs in bold
primary colors. Above her is the Holy Family consisting of a
free-standing large, red-smocked Mary wearing sandals and
cradling an infant Jesus whose smiling face peeps out from
under the aura of a purple halo. Behind them stands a pink
haloed Joseph carrying a shepherd's staff. The cross' arms sport,
alternately, a clustered village of one-room houses and a cluster
of smiling villagers beside an oversized ox and donkey, their
hatted heads turned reverently in the direction of the cradled
Christ child.

So many paradoxes here! The image of new life imprinted

upon the symbol of death, which mysteriously will lead to new life again. The Incarnation, the Crucifixion and the Resurrection fused in one. Sweet domestic contentment ushered in by a winged divine messenger, foreshadowing a horrifying death. The paradoxical faith of the Christian poor of El Salvador has sustained them through decades of unspeakable economic and political oppression. Tenderness amidst terror: the face of redemptive Love smiling out from the aura of a purple halo cradled in a mother's arms upon the cross-bars of the wood where nails and thorns will later do the affixing. The manifestation of a Love that shatters death.

So passionately does God embrace humankind, delight in us and find existence impossible without us, that no conditions can be put on the quest to bring us back into the divine embrace. Even the horrors of hell cannot separate us from the love God reveals to us on the cross. But hell does not triumph. Love does. And God, by giving up everything for us—even life itself—gives us the fullness of life in return.

★   ★   ★

In mid-September both the Western and Eastern church calendars make note of the liturgical feast of the Triumph of the Cross.[65] The traditional scripture readings for the observance situate the Calvary event in the context of salvation history. We are transported back to the time of Moses and the Hebrew people who wander in the desert.

> *From Mount Hor they set out by the way to the Red Sea, to go around the land of Edom; but the people became impatient on the way. The people spoke against God and against Moses, "Why have you brought us up out of Egypt to die in wilderness? For there is no food and no water, and we detest this miserable food." Then the LORD sent poisonous serpents among the people, and they bit the*

*people, so that many Israelites died. The people came to Moses and
said, "We have sinned by speaking against the* LORD *and against
you; pray to the* LORD *to take away the serpents from us." So
Moses prayed for the people. And the* LORD *said to Moses, "Make
a poisonous serpent, and set it on a pole; and everyone who is bit-
ten shall look at it and live." So Moses made a serpent of bronze,
and put it upon a pole; and whenever a serpent bit someone, that
person would look at the serpent of bronze and live.*

(NUMBERS 21:4–9)

This lifting up is a presage of the later lifting up that God will
effect. Reaching down, as it were, into the depths of human suffering, into the crucible of humanity's inhumanity, into the anguish of a world that would seek to obliterate God's presence, into
the hell of seeming abandonment, reaching down into the hidden caverns of the world's heart, God lifts up. God's beloved children are lifted up too.

*Let the same mind be in you that was in Christ Jesus,
who, though he was in the form of God,
did not regard equality with God
as something to be exploited,
but emptied himself
    taking the form of a slave,
being born in human likeness.
And being found in human form,
    he humbled himself,
and become obedient to the point of death—
even death on a cross.*

*Therefore God also highly exalted him
    and gave him the name
    that is above every name,*

so that at the name of Jesus
    every knee should bend,
in heaven and on earth and under the earth,
and every tongue confess that
Jesus Christ is Lord,
    to the glory of God the Father.

(PHILIPPIANS 2:5–11)

The observance is old. It began in 325 when the true cross was processed at the dedication of the churches at the site of the Holy Sepulchre and at Calvary in Jerusalem. Equally as old is the deep veneration given to the mysterious cross-armed pieces of wood which bore the weight of Jesus' bleeding body: this tree of death that ultimately became a blossoming tree of life. A tenth century liturgical manuscript records for us this prayer for the feast.

Holy Cross
You are more exalted than all the trees of the forest:
on you hung the life of the world;
on you Christ proceeded to his triumph;
on you death overcame death.[66]

And from the sixth-century Latin poet Venantius Fortunatus, chaplain at the monastic community of former Frankish Queen Rhadegunda and creator of some of the most wonderful of ancient Christian prayers, comes the *Vexilla Regis*.

The royal banners forward go, the cross shines forth in mystic glow,
Where he through whom our flesh was made, in that same flesh our
    ransom paid.
Fulfilled is all now what David told in true prophetic song of old;
How God the nations' King should be, for God is reigning from the tree.

O tree of glory, tree most fair, ordained those holy limbs to bear:
Gone is thy shame, each crimsoned bough proclaims the King of
glory now.
Blest tree, whose chosen branches bore the wealth that did the world
restore.
The price of humankind to pay to spoil the spoiler of his prey.
O cross, our one reliance, hail! Still may your power with us avail
to save us sinners from our sin, God's righteousness for all to win.
To thee, eternal Three in One, lot homage meet by all be done;
As by the cross thou dost restore so rule and guide us every more.[67]

The power of the cross excited the imagination of early Christians. Legend has it that in the fourth century Helena, mother of Emperor Constantine and a devout Christian, went on pilgrimage to the Holy Land in search of remaining fragments of the cross. When her team of excavators had unearthed their buried treasures, they found the remains of three crosses. The question of how to determine which were the authentic fragments was solved when a deceased boy was carried by on a bier. Touched with one of the fragments of the crosses, the dead child suddenly raised up. Thus were the fragments of the true cross discovered. To what does this rather curious legend point? I think it underscores the deep belief in the power of the cross, a belief fundamental to Christianity: that the power of God's love is greater than any other power, even death itself. Transformation is possible. Jean Valjean, the thief, can become a just and merciful man. What is most desperate and lost of human experience can become the forge of grace.

The truth revealed here is that the pathway of transformation paradoxically runs directly through the pain and brokenness of the world. God's love is not limited to those who would shun all that is joyously human in fear of taking on worldly corruption. Nor is grace a stranger to the sorrowful and twisted labyrinths of the human heart. The power of that cross—hung love confounds our sensibilities and plunges us into the whirlpool of paradox.

★   ★   ★

From the point of view of common sensibilities, it is perhaps a bewildering fact that the earliest Christian calendars were constructed around the observances of the deaths of those who died in imitation of and in participation with the carpenter-prophet of Nazareth who died so ignominiously on a cross in Roman-occupied Judea. Those death-days were, of course, observed joyously, as births to new life. The early church honored its martyrs mightily, saw in them second Christs who in their own flesh continued the powerful resurrection energy that was believed to be flooding the cosmos. The martyrs were thought to go to the right hand of God where they acted as intercessors for those who remained in the earthly community. Everything associated with the martyrs was for the early believers changed with sacred power—their bones, their belongings, the tombs where their bodies were laid. Those tombs were the gathering places of the nascent church, the sacred sites where the first love feasts were reenacted, the theaters in which the oral narrative tradition of Christianity was first performed. The story could not be told too often. Through death, death itself had been vanquished, a power greater than all endings, diminishments, defeats, and grief had been unleashed. The tale was lovingly proclaimed. It came to life again and again in the men and women who offered their lives to the truth that even death is swallowed up in the immense ocean of divine love, that the ultimate terror of human existence becomes a puny player on the cosmic stage.

The liturgical calendar still marks the memorials of those martyred for their faith. In fact, in times past when Christians have pitted themselves against other Christians, all parties have drawn up their own martyrologies and we have recorded tales, all heroic, many sad, which speak to us of brave Catholic, Anabaptist, and Reformed witnesses who laid down their lives in the path of Christian fratricidal warfare. I hope these martyrs serve as cautionary figures who can enlarge and enliven our contemporary vision of ourselves as church.

Other martyrs met their ends while on evangelical missions to lands where Christianity was being newly introduced. We may wonder, with twentieth-century hindsight, about the meaning of mission. How do we preach a faith that does not diminish the integrity of other cultures' vision of ultimacy or seek to simply refashion other peoples in our own image? But these are twentieth-century questions born out of the crucible of interfaith dialogue and the experience of the global village. The fact remains that the martyrs' message to us, no matter what the historical perimeters that enclosed their lives, goes beyond the particulars of the truth they proclaimed, the specific interpretation of doctrine current in their day, or the way they viewed the faith in relation to other religious traditions. The foundational intimation that the martyrs' witness conveys is the intimation of the cross: the power of divine love to transfigure reality.

Martyrs' memorials punctuate the liturgical calendar throughout the year, but there are a cluster of fairly obscure observances on the Roman calendar concentrated in the month of September just after the Triumph of the Cross. These memorials illustrate the diversity of the witness that is revealed to us through the lives of the martyred. There is the commemoration of Pope Corneluis and of Bishop Cyprian, third-century correspondents who wrote to one another from their respective residences at Rome and Carthage.[68] Theirs was a Christian experience marked by persecution. We know most about Cyprian, a gifted rhetoritician, whose insightful writings on the church and ministry have survived. Fleeing from his diocese several times before he was finally martyred, Cyprian was active in clarifying church teaching on the practice of rebaptism.

Very different are saints Cosmas and Damian, twin brothers whose lives and martyrdoms are shrouded in the obscurity of legend. Their cult was well established as early as the fifth century, and they are remembered as two beneficent physicians who generously practiced their art without thought of renumeration.[69]

Another quite distinctive martyr is the equally obscure Januarius, Bishop of Benevento, who lost his life under the reign of terror instituted by the Roman Emperor Diocletian. Januarius's relics in Naples draw a crowd some eighteen times a year where a miraculous "liquefaction" of his blood is reputed to occur.[70]

More recent martyrs hail from Korea. Andrew Kim Taegon, Paul Chong Hasung, and their companions all died for their embrace of the Christian faith in the waves of persecution that swept through Korea in the nineteenth century.[71]

Each of these men, and the innumerable other women and men who are noted as martyrs throughout the liturgical year, speak to us as a community not only of their personal courage or heroic witness. They speak also to us of the triumph of the cross. For the days we set aside to honor them are not only death days, they are birth days. They teach us once again that it is love and not death that is the final word, the word that speaks us into the fullness of being at both ends of our little lives.

★   ★   ★

Clearly not all the saints memorialized on the Christian calendar are martyrs. Most are remembered for the quality of their lives rather than the specifics of their deaths. And, in the early centuries, most saints were designated as such by the popular proclamation of the community. Indeed, this is still the way that we unofficially "canonize" those in our midst whose lives are exemplary. Our global appreciation for the work of the late Mother Teresa of Calcutta is a case in point. Her tender, unstinting care for the poorest of the poor—the destitute dying among the slums of India—speaks profoundly to the conscience of a world in which human life is often seen as expendable. In the mind of the late twentieth century, Mother Teresa is a saint.

But this process of popular acclamation, as persistent as it has been, was clarified and centralized by the church as the centuries passed. During the medieval centuries it became the practice to search for saints that could have universal appeal. Most of those popularly acclaimed were local heros or heroines. Often they were revered because miracles and marvels had been attributed to them after their deaths. Sometimes these marvels were suspect. Sometimes there seemed nothing estimable in the way they had led their lives. So the process of official canonization was developed to hold up women and men within the faith community whose lives were universally exemplary. A variety of criteria were raised to determine who would be canonized. Exemplary works were important: founders of Christian communities, church leaders of note, articulate apologists for the faith, missionaries, those who tended the sick and dying, instructed the ignorant, or ministered to the faithful. Equally important was that the saints exhibit exemplary virtue.

What is virtue? Or more precisely, what are the virtues? Gradually the church worked out a list of those qualities of the person that seemed foundational to the Christian life. The list was sevenfold and included the three "theological virtues"—faith, hope, and charity—and the four "cardinal virtues"—prudence, temperance, fortitude, and justice. Saint Paul grouped together the first cluster of these (1 Corinthians 13:13, cf. 1 Thessalonians 1:3; Galatians: 5:5-6, Colossians 1:4-5) as the basis of the Christian life. The second cluster originally derived from the classifications of Plato and Aristotle. Saints throughout the medieval centuries were those who not only did good works or performed heroic actions, they also exhibited the virtues as well.

Too often today we think of virtuousness as a sort of self-important righteousness. People who are virtuous are "above it all." They think they're better than everyone else when in fact they are simply prudish and judgmental. Happily, we are beginning to see the virtues come into focus once again. Within the discipline of ethics, "virtue ethics" is gaining ground. The practice of the virtues has only secondarily to do with exemplary behavior. And it is not to be equated with correctly following all the rules. The virtues are habits of character sometimes innately possessed as "gifts," other times painfully cultivated over the years, which form the foundation for all actions and thoughts that flow from a person. To possess the virtue of hope, for example, is to have that deep buoyancy that continues to desire and search for the future good, confident in God's goodness in the face of all obstacles. The "vice" that corresponds to the virtue of hope would be despair.

Medieval moral theologians (notably Ambrose, Augustine, and Thomas Aquinas)[72] made much of the virtues and their cultivation. Aquinas especially insisted that the Christian life, while essentially a life of response to grace, involved our cooperation. Today we might say that conscious reflection on our gentle yet insistent efforts to shape our lives according to the promises we have been given is essential. I like to think of virtue not so much as particular virtuous acts as habits of character formed by our attentiveness. What does it mean to cultivate an underlying attitude of faith? Of hope? Of charity? Of prudence? Of temperance? Of fortitude? Of justice? Or are there other foundational qualities of character that we need to cultivate in today's world? Compassion? Solidarity? Simplicity?

The point here is that the Christian life, and that includes the spiritual life, is a process of consciously living into our true identity as beloved sons and daughters. There is a dying implied in the process, a dying to our false selves, to all that grips us and keeps us unfree, a dying so that we might be lifted up, free to flourish, free to love, free to witness to the mysterious power of Love that can transform the world.

Watching over Me

(Late September to Early October)

All night, all day,
Angels watchin' over me, my Lord,
All night, all day,
Angels watchin' over me[73]

CATHOLIC SCHOOLCHILDREN OF AN EARLIER GENERATION WERE taught, along with their ABC's, the Guardian Angel Prayer.

Angel of God, my guardian dear,
To whom God's love commits me here,
Ever this day be at my side,
To watch and guard, to rule and guide.

Each child learned that God had assigned to him or her an angel to be guardian and guide throughout life. A guardian angel was half conscience, half familiar companion, a little like Jiminy Cricket, scolding, advocating, and protecting his wooden-headed friend in the Disney version of *Pinocchio.*

A sense of invisible companions belongs not only to an older generation of Catholics or to newer generations of evangelical Christians and New Age practitioners. The world in which the New Testament came into being was steeped in a sense of hovering presences, especially angels. The gospel writers depict Jesus as surrounded by angels at the most crucial moments of his life: they announce his incarnation (Matthew 1:20, 24), and birth (Luke 2:9-15), minister to him in the desert (Matthew 4:11), strengthen him in his agony (Luke 22:43), would be ready to defend him at his capture (Matthew 26:53), and are the first witnesses to his resurrection (Matthew 28:2-7; John 20:12f). Accounts of angels appear throughout the Old and New Testaments. They are beings intermediate between humans and God. Some of their multitude form a holy court about God, others have an earthward mission.

It was Pseudo-Dionysius, the Areopagite, a sixth-century Christian who fixed the orders and numbers of angels in his "Celestial Hierarchies." These are the ranks of angels with which we are familiar today. From this adventurous contemplative thinker we get the three hierarchies containing three choirs each in the order of Seraphim, Cherubim, and Thrones; Dominations, Virtues, and Powers; Principalities, Archangels, and Angels of whom we sing in our traditional hymns and speak in our hallowed prayers. Of all the choirs only Dionysius's last two have a mission to human beings. It is those, the earth-bound messengers, that have especially captured the imagination of Christian generations.

Among the messengers that have captured our fancy, the archangels Michael, Gabriel, and Raphael have taken on personality and character.[74] Michael is known as captain of the angelic hosts; he appears in iconography as a sword-slinging, dragon-slaying warrior triumphing over the forces of evil. Gabriel is the messenger of divine comfort who assists Daniel in understanding his visions, foretells the birth of John the Baptist, and announces Jesus' conception to Mary. Raphael's name in Hebrew means "God has healed" and legend has it that the archangel healed the earth defiled by the sins of fallen angels. All the archangels are said to surround God's throne.

A sense of being surrounded with loving presence is an integral feature of the Christian life. We do not envision a bare, friendless universe where men and women strive alone. Rather, grace suffuses all that is, seeping down into the farthest recesses of pain and isolation, encouraging, supporting, and drawing us into the embrace of Love. For some of us, this pervasive presence takes the form of hovering angels. For others of us the communion of saints is an enveloping energy that encircles us. For still others it is Jesus as friend or brother or loved one who walks by our sides. For all of us, there are others, not invisible but visible, who provide the encircling presence so necessary for us to continue. For we cannot travel alone.

These encircling visible presences come to us with many faces. The most obvious is the local congregation or parish church. It is with the local community that we celebrate the cycle of seasons that make up the Christian story. In the worship of the local community we learn to weave the great stories of faith into the fabric of our little lives. But often the companionship of the worshiping community is not enough. We need as well smaller circles of care to provide support, encouragement, and presence.

Christians have done such companioning for one another from the very beginning. The earliest churches were house churches that provided hospitality, friendship, and faith support in an intimate setting. But even when the church grew and some of the intimacy of the first communities was lost, women and men sought one another out. To be known by name, to know another, to share the journey was essential. The history of the church is in part the story of those small community movements that have arisen over and over again: the "spiritual marriages" of the first centuries, chaste friendships between women and men contracted for the purpose of spiritual growth; the master-disciple relationships of seekers and the ascetic *abbas* and *ammas* of the desert; the house asceticism of early Roman matrons; the soul friendships of the Celtic church; the medieval Beguine movement comprised of women who joined together in pursuit of piety and good works; the fourteenth-century "modern devotion" movement comprised of devout laypersons, monastics, and clerics; the Pietist circles within Lutheranism; the clusters of devotees who gathered around medieval holy women like Julian of Norwich and Angela of Foligno; the band societies of nascent Wesleyanism; Bible study and faith-sharing groups in the contemporary era. The list could expand endlessly. The point is, while there is an essential solitude about the spiritual life, it is never a life cut off from the equally essential nourishment of community. It is a life open to the realization of our interdependence.

Catherine of Siena, the notable fourteenth-century holy woman about whom clustered a throng of spiritual disciples, wrote in *The Dialogue* of the profound interconnection among those who belong to the body of Christ. Catherine painted a word picture of the church as a vast vineyard in which each of us has our own discreet vineyard. Yet none of the separate plots, while they remain distinctive, is fenced off from the others.

> *You then, are my workers. You have come from me, the supreme eternal gardener, and I have engrafted you onto the vine by making myself one with you.*

> *Keep in mind that each of you has your own vineyard. But every one is joined to your neighbor's vineyard without any dividing lines, they are so joined together, in fact, that you cannot do good or evil for yourself without doing the same for your neighbors.*

> *All of you together make up one common vineyard of the mystic body of holy Church from which you draw your life. In this vineyard is planted the vine which is my only-begotten Son, into whom you must be engrafted.*[75]

The nurturant biblical imagery of the vine and branches is extended by Catherine to its logical conclusion. We do not go to God alone. We go with and through one another.

It is, of course, often our families who are the first nurturers of our faith and it is through the common tasks of caretaking,

providing, and homemaking that we become consciously en-
grafted onto the vine of God's love. But as we grow we reach out
to a more intentional family of persons who will continue to
water, weed, and prune our vineyard. The second half of the
twentieth century has seen an explosion of small intentional spiritual groupings within the Christian communion that have taken
on the tasks of being guardians and gardeners for one another.
Two specific forms of spiritual companionship, among many, arrest my attention. The first is the widespread practice of spiritual
direction. The second is the phenomenon of liberation base communities.

Spiritual direction or as some prefer to call it, spiritual guidance, midwifing, or holy listening, is an ancient spiritual art that
has blossomed in our present day. The art of listening attentively
with another to the prompting of the Spirit has its origins in the
early community and over the centuries has taken many forms.
In the present ecumenical climate spiritual direction is generally
practiced as a one-on-one relationship in which the "director" or
"listener" focuses lovingly on the unfolding narrative provided by
the "directee" and, in a manner that respects autonomy and indi-
viduality, helps the directee to perceive more clearly where God
is moving in her or his life. The true relationship in this form of
companionship is not two-way but three-way. God is the true
director and the listener, a facilitator of the central relationship
between the directee and God.

This intentional form of companionship is related but not
identical to spiritual friendship, which is more mutual, equal, less
formal, and often less intentional than direction. Friendships simply occur. Spiritual direction is consciously sought out. More and
more, persons with an awakening sense of the centrality of the
spiritual life are seeking directors or listeners to accompany them
on the way. Not all pastors or priests are skilled in this ministry,
although some are, and not all skilled directors are to be found
on the premises of church property or among the ordained.

Rather Christians gifted with discernment, wisdom, and self-knowledge, prompted by a call and educated in the arts of spiritual accompaniment are, with frequency, offering their gifts to the community.

Margaret Guenther, a contemporary Episcopalian gifted in the art of spiritual direction writes:

> *For me, spiritual direction is always storytelling. I don't mean that we move doggedly through the directee's life, year by year and decade by decade. The story moves around in time, gliding or leaping from present to past, from present to future. Without the story, there is no flesh, no blood, no specificity. But I find that it doesn't matter where we begin. It is always a story of a journey, always a story about relationship with God—whether the directee is fleeing the Hound of Heaven, or lost, or yearning, or living among the swine and eating their husks.*

> *The director's task is to help connect the individual's story to the story and thereby help the directee to recognize and claim identity in Christ, discern the action of the Holy Spirit. There is a God-component in all human experience, even in lives that seem pain-filled and remote from God. A sense of God's absence or remorse at one's own inattentiveness to God's presence can be a fruitful place for beginning direction. However the story is structured, it eventually includes fragments of the story from the past, the present, and the future. . . .*

> *The fact of being entrusted with someone's soul, of being allowed to enter the story, however layered and convoluted it might be, is staggering. Fortunately, there is yet another surprise in store for the spiritual director. Like Sarah baking the cakes or the unnamed servant dressing the calf, the director is a necessary, but distinctly secondary figure in the offering of hospitality. Without warning, the role of host, of Guest Giver, is preempted! This should not be surprising, for the*

gospels offer precedents: Jesus had a way of taking over at the din-
ner table. So too in the ministry of spiritual direction—when all is
said and done, the Holy Spirit is the true director. I find this reas-
suring when I am overcome by performance anxiety. Will I be wise?
Will I be sufficiently holy, or at least look that way? Will I do even
a half-way decent job? But if I am ready to relinquish my role to
the true Host, the burden of responsibility drops away and the space
I have prepared becomes gracious and holy.[76]

Another uniquely twentieth-century form of spiritual companioning can be discovered in the Latin American churches.
"Base communities" have emerged among the poor and power-
less in countries laboring under the burdens of social and political oppression and economic misery. For centuries the gospel was
identified with the culture of the European colonizers. The
landowners, the rich, and those who governed had brought the
good news to Latin American soil. The conquered people had received and embraced that news. Their embrace was wide and
their hearing of that news clear. Gradually, the masses who more
and more came to have little, while their conquerors gained
much, began to hear the gospel as if it were directed precisely to
them. No longer did they believe that God waited for them in
some future ideal life earned by their patient suffering below.
They came to believe that God did not intend them to suffer injustice in this world. They were not rightly exploited, impoverished, and disregarded by the wealthy and powerful. God
intended all people to live with dignity. They began to gather together in small Christian communities to read the gospel as a
message of liberation for the poor.

There was a rich man who was dressed in purple and fine linen
and who feasted sumptuously every day. And at his gate lay a poor
man named Lazarus, covered with sores, who longed to satisfy his
hunger with what fell from the rich man's table; even the dogs would

*come and lick his sores. The poor man died and was carried away
by the angels to be with Abraham. The rich man also died and was
buried. In Hades, where he was being tormented, he looked up and
saw Abraham far away with Lazarus by his side. He called out,
"Father Abraham, have mercy on me, and send Lazarus to dip the
tip of his finger in water and cool my tongue; for I am in agony in
these flames." But Abraham said, "Child, remember that during your
lifetime you received your good things, and Lazaras in like manner
evil things; but now he is comforted here, and you are in agony."
Besides this all this, between you and us a great has been fixed, so
that those who might wish to pass from here to you cannot do so,
and no one can cross from there to us. He said, "Then, father, I beg
you to send him to my father's house—for I have five brothers—that
he may warn them, that they will not also come into this place of
torment." Abraham replied, "They have Moses and the prophets;
they should listen to them." He said, "No, father Abraham; but if
someone goes to them from the dead, they will repent. He said to
him, "If they do not listen to Moses and the prophets, neither will
they be convinced even if someone rises form the dead."*

(LUKE 16:19-32)

At Solentiname, Nicaragua, in the seventies in a base community that included Ernesto Cardencel, a catechist, and local
townspeople, the liberating discussion of the parable of the rich
man took this turn:

FELIPE: "I think the poor man here stands for all the poor,
and the rich man for all the rich. The poor man is saved and
the rich man is damned. That's the story, a very simple one,
that Jesus tells us."

GLORIA: "The rich man's sin was that he had no compassion. Poverty was at his door, and that didn't disturb him at his parties."

WILLIAM: "The traditional interpretation of this passage is wrong and is used for exploitation; because the poor man has been led to believe that he must patiently endure because after death he's going to be better off and that the rich will get their punishment."

FELIPE: "As I see it, this passage was rather to threaten the rich so they wouldn't go on exploiting; but it seems it turned out the opposite: it served to pacify the people."

OLIVIA: "I think the word of God has been very badly preached, and the church is much to blame in this. It's because the Gospel hasn't been well preached that we have a society still divided between rich and poor. There are few places like Solentiname where the Gospel is preached and we understand it. Also, it's we poor people who understand it. Unfortunately, the rich don't come to hear it. Where the rich are, there's no preaching like that."

MARIITA: "The rich man's sin was not sharing—not sharing with everybody, that is, with the poor, too; because he did share with the rich: the Gospel says he gave parties every day."

JULIO: "They weren't inviting the poor; they'd get their houses dirty."

ERNESTO: "I believe this parable was not to console the poor but rather to threaten the rich; but as you said, William, it has had the opposite effect, because the rich weren't going to heed it. But Christ himself is saying that in this parable: that the rich pay no attention to the Bible."

OSCAR: "It seems like it doesn't do any good to be reading the Bible, then, because if you don't want to change the social order, you might as well be reading any damned thing, you might as well be reading any stupid book."

ERNESTO: "It seems to me that Jesus' principal message is that the rich aren't going to be convinced even with the . Bible, not even with a dead man coming to life—and not even with Jesus' resurrection."[77]

★   ★   ★

It was the prosperity of the church, anchored as it was in the exploitation of slave labor, that began to trouble John Woolman's conscience. The eighteenth-century Quaker tailor and preacher could not close his eyes to what his fellow Quakers in the American colonies took for granted. Woolman had an almost mystical sense of the reality of the Inner Light, the inward divine presence that the Society of Friends believed was accessible to all people. The prompting of the Light urged him into a bold ministry of action. In the most conciliatory manner imaginable he journeyed from local Friends meeting to meeting, gently raising his "concern" that no person should profit from the degration or exploitation of another. The prosperous land- and slaveholders he visited had never abused their slaves, but Woolman held before them the troubling question of ownership. Can one in conscience "own" another human being? His ministry substantially reduced slave ownership among Friends in Pennsylvania and New Jersey.

John Woolman is among my favorite encircling presences, persons whose extraordinary embrace of the good news challenges and comforts me. The Calendar of Commemoration for United Methodists officially remembers him October 7. His memorial falls in the stretch of time in the liturgical year between September 29 and October 15 when I feel most powerfully aware of the hovering presences of the great saints. Marvelous and inspiring figures populate the church calendar all through the year, but the fortnight that spans September's end and October's beginning is electric with my beloved saints.

On the Roman calendar October 1 is reserved for Thérèse of Lisieux, the "Little Flower," a French nun who died of tuberculosis in 1897 at the tender age of twenty-four in an obscure Carmelite convent. It was not until after her death and the publication of her autobiography (written at the request of her superiors) that Thérèse's "little way" of spirituality became known. Fired with great desire to attain heroic sanctity, Thérèse was nonetheless aware of her immaturity and weakness. She chose instead to put all her confidence in the One who is holiness itself, and launching out of her heart toward God in prayer, she uttered cries of grateful love from both the crest of joy and the trough of despair. Her secret was to remain very little and trust utterly in God. Thérèse was barely noticed by many of her sisters in monastic life, yet she set her mind to accomplish all her actions, even the most insignificant, with immense love. Her "little" way of patience, simplicity, and unwavering courtesy has earned her the recent application in the Catholic world of "Doctor of the Church."

Thérèse is not the only saint who witnesses to the mysterious power of littleness. On October 4 virtually all the Western calendars make note of Francis of Assisi, the most well known of Christian saints. In the popular mind, Francis is associated with the celebration of the natural world. Indeed, his "Canticle of Brother Sun" has engraved itself deeply in the hearts of the current generation. We sing paraphrases of his canticle in our worship services,

All creatures of our God and King,
  Lift up your voice and with us sing;
  Alleluia! Alleluia!
  O burning sun with golden beam
  And silver moon with softer gleam:
  O praise him! O praise him!
  Alleluia, Alleluia,
  Alleluia![78]

Francis did witness in ecstatic love to the wonder of the creation. For this, he has been designated the patron saint of ecology. But the man from Assisi is much more than the charming birdbath portrayals of him suggest. He was a man gripped in the vise of God's mysterious, self-emptying love.

As a youth, Francis (which means "free") gave himself over to the social pleasures of his affluent thirteenth-century urban life but, after a brief term of military service, imprisonment, illness, and a prophetic dream, he became dissatisfied and began to devote time to prayer and service of the poor. On a pilgrimage to Rome, moved by the sight of the poor begging before Saint Peter's, he exchanged clothes with one of them and he himself begged for alms. The experience left a permanent mark. Francis came to believe and know the love of God manifest through the poverty of Christ. The vulnerability of the baby in the manger, the itinerancy of the man who had no place to lay his head, the abandonment of the one who died naked on the cross: the unspeakable poverty of God's own life in the world possessed him. Francis embraced his love: "Lady Poverty," he called her. Going barefoot, clothed in a single rough robe, owning nothing, he had no spiritual or material riches, no position, no titles, no degrees, nothing that could separate him from the poverty he beheld in God, Francis founded a movement called the Friars Minor, the littlest brothers (the Franciscan order). His growing interior likeness to the cross-hung Christ culminated toward the end of his life when, in an ecstatic experience, his hands, feet, and side were imprinted with wounds such as those that marked the body of Christ.

Teresa of Avila is the fourth of the holy luminaries that adorn the calendar in this late part of the liturgical year. Like Thérèse of Lisieux, she is known in the Roman communion as Doctor of the Church. Like Francis, she was the founder of a religious group. Or, more precisely, she was the vigorous reformer of the sixteenth-century Carmelite order to which she belonged. Teresa, whose memorial is placed on October 15, has become a favorite subject of twentieth-century scholarship. Her long, rather ordinary life as a cloistered religious figure was transformed when she was in midlife. Contemplative intimacy with Christ emboldened her to embark on a massive reform of her order, returning to the austerity of its primitive rule and wresting control of her communities out of the hands of the Spanish aristocracy who were traditional monastic patrons. Teresa was a feisty woman whom I like to think of as trudging up and down the treacherous byways of Spain at an age when most women would be enjoying their grandchildren. It is said of her that once, her rough-hewn carriage having broken down in the mud during a torrential downpour and finding herself stranded at night miles from lodging or human help, Teresa wryly commented to the Divine Companion who encouraged all her journeys, "Well, if this is the way you treat your friends, I'd like to see how you treat your enemies."

This remarkable woman of action was also a woman of profound prayer. Indeed, prayer was the source of her action. Teresa is known for her epoch-making descriptions of the subtle dynamics of the spiritual journey, describing states of prayer intermediate between discursive mediation and ecstasy.

Each of my favored saints seems especially present during this time of the year. They create a hovering sense of presence into which I enter with delight.

★   ★   ★

The saint from Avila can be remembered for many things. Among these is a paraphrase and translation of a prayer that she is said to have treasured:

> Christ has no body here but yours,
> No arms, no hands, no feet.
> He has only your arms, your hands, your feet.

If a recitation of the exploits of the memorable saintly who have lived among us in the past seems beside the point to us in the present, I would suggest that it is not simply the particulars of their lives that commend them to us. How many of us will found or renew religious orders, write an autobiography, or become wandering beggars or preachers? Rather, they are memorable because these women and men allowed their lives to be invaded by Love itself. They genuinely lived their faith. They knew they were Christ's living body.

Throughout the centuries of the church's existence it has been assumed that all Christians could genuinely live their faith. And past eras have not been quite so mystified as we seem to be about what that living might look like. The Christian life was encapsulated in the traditional "Works of Mercy." There were fourteen enumerated in all: seven corporal works of mercy and seven spiritual works of mercy. The former were deduced with some additions from the twenty-fifth chapter of Matthew. To feed the hungry, give drink to the thirsty, cloth the naked, minister to the imprisoned, visit the sick, shelter the homeless, and bury the dead: these were the mandates for the bodily care of others. The spiritual works of mercy ran parallel: admonish the sinner, instruct the ignorant, counsel the doubtful, comfort the sorrowful, bear wrongs patiently, forgive injuries, and pray for the living and the dead.?

The practice of the corporal works of mercy seems to have developed in the early church when baptism was thought to confer a perfect transformation in the one receiving the sacrament. The difficulty of how to respond when baptized Christians committed grievous and public sins or when, under persecution, they recanted their faith and yet in stabler times wanted to be readmitted to the community of the faithful, gave rise to the need for public penance. Such penance could wash away the stain that marred baptismal innocence. Undertaking the tasks of feeding the hungry, clothing the naked, and so forth were the approved means by which innocence was restored.

Gradually the works of mercy lost their compensatory function and became instead the expected norms by which the Christian life was measured. The medieval world saw them as implied in the life that began with baptism. They were the work of those who were Christ's arms, Christ's feet, and Christ's heart in the world.

Perhaps it is the excessive individualism of our age or the fact that we live in a culture in which so many choices are possible, but I sometimes wonder if we are the wallflowers of the great Christian dance of holiness. We are waiting for our "real" call, for the job or ministry or artistic expression that will tap our untapped creativity and liberate all our gifts when all around us are opportunities to practice the works of mercy. In our homes, in our families, among our colleagues, in our congregations, in our neighborhoods. Feed those who are hungry. Shelter the stranger. Visit the sick. Minister to prisoners. Bury the dead. Convert sinners. Instruct the ignorant. Counsel the doubtful. Comfort the sorrowing. Bear wrongs patiently. Forgive injuries. Pray for others.

It is not necessary to sense the presence of angels or to feel the encircling energy of the communion of saints to live into the reality that someone is watching over us. We can become presence for one another. We can be the arms, the legs, the feet, the heart of Christ in the world.

Rising Like Incense

(Late October)

Day is done, but love unfailing
Dwells ever here;
Shadows fall, but hope, prevailing,
Calms every fear.
God, our maker, none forsaking,
Take our hearts, of Love's own making,
Watch our sleeping, guard our waking,
Be always near.[80]

MY HUSBAND AND OUR TWO YOUNGEST, AT THE TIME IN THEIR teens, piled into a fifteen-foot rental truck and once again made the familiar four-hour trip on the narrow two-lane highways that run north-south between Nebraska and Kansas. This time their plans were different. Instead of a summer weekend's visit to celebrate Grandma June's birthday and take a refreshing dip in her apartment building's swimming pool or a jaunt to participate in one of Dad's frequent high school class reunions or a quick winter trip to gather Grandma and her carefully wrapped presents (mainly Avon products) into the car for the drive to our house and a Christmas celebration, they were going to dismantle her apartment. Now ninety-three and having lived independently for almost thirty years since Grandpa Frank's death, she was moving out. Five weeks previously she had slipped on a kitchen throw rug, bruised herself, and suffered hairline fractures to two ribs. Her habitual refusal to consider living in any other circumstance than her independent one gave way. Her son and grandchildren found themselves in the unfamiliar setting of a nursing facility

183

and Grandma, who until two weeks before had enjoyed a twice-weekly bridge game, a monthly P.E.O. chapter meeting (a philanthropic organization), weekly church attendance and visits to the hairdresser's and grocery store, occasional outings to Kansas State University musical concerts or theater productions (season basketball tickets had been recently relinquished), and frequent appearances (as the oldest living junior high faculty member) at school reunions and town meetings, was less primly dressed and neatly coiffed than they were used to seeing her.

All things wax and all things wane. As a novagenarean, my mother-in-law in some eyes may be well past the evening of her life. But she has not followed anyone's typical pattern and her last thirty years have had the quality of eventide with their gentle, slightly relaxing rhythm, their savoring of the fruits of a life well lived.

It is not possible to make a chronological assessment of the eveningtide of a life, for people's lives vary so. But perhaps some obvious markers are, if one has been in the work force, retirement from full-time work or, if one has been primarily a homemaker, the time when the last child establishes a home of his or her own. Empty nests and Monday mornings without a six A.M. wake-up alarm present new possibilities for the person entering the evening of life. The classical Hindu tradition divides the human life cycle into various phases and envisions specific tasks for each phase. After the "householding" phase, which involves raising a family and cultivating a career or job that can provide for the family, is the "retirement" or "forest dweller" phase. While we in the United States tend to think of retirement in terms of sun-belt climate zones, golf courses, arts and crafts classes, travel in the forms of ocean cruises and recreational vehicles, or just enjoying the "good life," the Hindu tradition thinks instead of retirement as an especially spiritual phase of life.

Caretaking, providing, and laboring are activities of the householding years. In retirement a devout Hindu will typically give over a family business to an offspring and begin to simplify, leaving finances, property, and goods to the care of the younger generation. Retirement is the time to direct focused attention to the deep questions of human life. It is a time to withdraw somewhat and turn one's face in the direction of the divine. This phase is sometimes called the "forest dweller" phase because, in the evening of life, devout Hindus might well have dispossessed themselves of all the burdens of the householding years and gone off into the forest to seek ultimate spiritual liberation.

I am not suggesting that retreating to a desert or deserted mountaintop is the only or even the preferred way to celebrate the evening of life, but I am suggesting that there is, or can be, a spiritual richness to the waning years that is not well captured in our Western collective images of retirement as simply unfettered leisure time to golf and travel. Rather, we can be freed somewhat to ask ourselves what really matters, to give our energies to vital worthwhile causes we did not have time for previously, to attend to the movement of the Spirit in our hearts and in our world.

With some frequency I meet women and men who are inspiring examples of eveningtide living. A former executive of a major railroad company had taken early retirement and now donated his time to be financial advisor to the Unitarian church of which he was a member as well as to actively promote the work of Amnesty International, the human rights organization. I worked alongside him at the local Omaha chapter of Amnesty and was always extraordinarily gratified for his expertise and the gift of his time. The rest of the chapter members were full-time workers and/or full-time parents and we could give only limited time and talent to the cause we knew to be so vital. The group could not have functioned without the retired railroad executive's unstinting generosity.

Another woman I know in California decided in the evening of her life to pursue a new path. She, a lifelong elementary school teacher, and her husband, an accountant, had raised five children when she determined that she wanted to advocate for the poor. And the best way to do that seemed to be as a lawyer. So my midlife friend began to study law. She took one year of formal classes and then studied for several years on her own. This was in California where prospective lawyers sweat blood for years in grueling law school programs only to fail the bar exam three or four times before finally passing. My virtually self-taught school-teacher friend passed the bar on the first try. Then she went to work in a free legal clinic where people with fixed or small incomes came to be represented or advised in their legal concerns.

Not everyone in the evening years of life chooses such an active path. Contemplative hours spent gardening or tending the soil, joyous hours spent lavishing attention on grandchildren, companionate hours spent visiting the homebound, or quiet hours spent in prayer: all these and many more possibilities exist. In any case, the eveningtide of life can have a special quality. Easeful, generous, less hurried and worried than the householding years, it can bear ripe and nourishing fruit in which the entire community can share.

★   ★   ★

The Christian community has long recognized the particular quality of evening and has hallowed that daily time in prayer. The custom has roots in Jewish practice for the thrice-daily rhythm of ritual prayers is much older than the church. Be that as it may, the prayer at the waning of the sunlight has developed into the most elaborate and beautiful of the liturgical hours that mark the passage of the day—vespers or evening prayer. Its special characteristics are the use of light and incense.

A large lighted candle carried into the prayer space illuminates the dimming light of eventide. The prayer leader proclaims:

Jesus Christ is the light of the world.
And the gathered community responds:

the light no darkness can overcome.

They repeat the antiphonal pattern:

*Stay with us, Lord, for it is evening
and the day is almost over.
Let your light scatter the darkness
and illumine your church.*[81]

Then the ancient hymn to Christ the Light, *Phos Hilaron*, which dates from the third century, is sung.

*O radiant Light, O Sun divine,
of God the Father's deathless face,
O image of the Light sublime
that fills the heavenly dwelling place.*

*O Son of God, the source of life,
praise is your due by night and day.
Our happy lips must raise the strain
of your esteemed and splendid name.*

*Lord Jesus Christ, as daylight fades,
as shine the lights of eventide,
we praise the Father with the Son,
the Spirit blest and with them one.*[82]

Brief prayers of praise then lead into Psalm 141, "incense psalm," most associated with the evening office. The community prays as the sweet fragrance of incense is allowed to fill the worship space, cleansing, beautifying, and linking heaven and earth with a column of fragrance.

*O Lord, I call to you; come to me quickly;
hear my voice when I cry to you.*

Let my prayer be set forth in your sight as incense,
*   the lifting of my hands as the evening sacrifice.*

Set a watch before my mouth, O Lord,
and guard the door of my lips;
*   let not my heart incline to any evil thing*

Let me not be occupied in wickedness with evildoers,
*   nor eat of their choice foods.*

Let the righteous smite me in friendly rebuke;
let not the oil of the unrighteous anoint my head;
*   for my prayer is continually against their evil deeds.*

. . . .

But my eyes are turned to you, Lord God;
*   in you I take refuge;*
*   do not strip me of my life.*

Protect me from the snare which they have laid for me
*   and from the trap of evildoers.*

Let the wicked fall into their own nets,
*   while I myself escape.*

Holy God,
let the incense of our prayer ascend before you,
and let your loving-kindness descend upon us,'
that with devoted hearts we may sing your praise
with the church on earth and the whole heavenly host,
and glorify you forever and ever. Amen.

(Psalm 141 is from *An Inclusive-Language Psalter of the Christian People*)

In the evening we slow our pace. Our vigorous daylight labor has ceased. The setting sun invites us to gentle ourselves, to return home, to enjoy the fruits of our work. The ancient office likewise invites us to savor the delicious moments of letting go when we turn attention away from our labors and toward the source of our life. We begin the day in praise and petition and so we greet the approach of its end.

It is a wonderful thing to be mindful of the natural rhythms of the earth and of our bodies. Our contemporary, artificially illuminated, round-the-clock busy lives may have increased our economic productivity, but they have also robbed us of our sensitivity to the restorative alternating rhythms of labor followed by rest. The waning hours of the day with the magic of gathering darkness are unlike any other hours. They are gentle, expansive, and full of peace. The prayers of the vesper liturgy reflect these qualities.

Come upon us with quietness and still our souls,
that we may listen for the whisper of your Spirit
and be attentive to your nearness in our dreams.

. . . .

Calm our souls,
and refresh us with your peace.

. . . .

To you, O God,
we surrender ourselves,
trusting our risen Lord to lead us always
in the way of peace.[83]

Each of the daily offices includes one of the New Testament canticles, those ancient songs incorporated into the text that were beloved by the early community. The canticle recited at vespers is always the "Magnificat," the hymn of rejoicing that Luke places in the mouth of the young, newly pregnant Mary. The "Magnificat" is the song of one who knows God is with her, the joyful utterance of one who has reached down into the deepest longing discoverable in the heart of humankind and found the presence of a saving, liberating God.

Tell out, my soul, the greatness of the Lord,
rejoice, rejoice, my spirit, in God my savior;
so tenderly has he looked upon his servant,
*   humble as she is.*
For, from this day forth,
all generations will count me blessed,
so wonderfully has he dealt with me,
*   the Lord, the Mighty One.*

His name is Holy;
his mercy sure from generation to generation
*   toward those who fear him;*
the deeds his own right arm has done
*   disclose his might:*
the arrogant of heart and mind he has put to rout,
he has brought down monarchs from their thrones,
*   but the humble have been lifted high.*
The hungry he has satisfied with good things,
*   the rich sent empty away.*

He has ranged himself at the side of Israel his servant;
*   firm in his promise to our forefathers,*
he has not forgotten to show mercy to Abraham
*   and his children's children, for ever.'*

(LUKE 1:46–55, NEB)

Mary's song is the song of the entire church, filled with the fruit of the promises that have echoed down the centuries; promises of a world renewed, hope fulfilled, the dearest longings of the human heart, for peace, justice, and tenderness to pervade all life.

I personally find Mary to be one of the most compelling figures that emerge for us from the biblical text and have taken on personality over centuries of Christian devotion. As a biblical figure she is, of course, the mother of Jesus. And she is a symbol of Israel's prophetic hope for a transformed world. Throughout the centuries, both ordinary believers and theologians have found themselves following out the implications of Mary's motherhood. They have prayed with her as she heard the greeting of the angel Gabriel, stood awestruck with her at the side of the crib, been amazed with her at her son's miracles at the wedding of Cana, agonized with her at the foot of the cross, and have felt with her the mighty gust of the Spirit's descent at Pentecost. As they accompanied her, she became a living presence to them.

Clearly, in the years of the Protestant reformation, as reformers sought to root Christian practice in apostolic soil, much of the Mary story that had become part of Christendom's symbolic world was abandoned. Yet the Roman rite and, to a great extent, the Anglican-Episcopalian traditions have retained Mary as a fuller figure than the young Jewish girl who was Jesus' mother. Interestingly, there is something of a resurgence of interest in Marian devotions among many Protestants interested in spirituality today. I have discovered many theologically sophisticated United Methodist, United Church of Christ, and Presbyterian Christians who pray the rosary.

Be that as it may, in the Roman rite, Mary is amply celebrated. Vespers in any denomination contain the "Magnificat." In Roman practice, the entire service seems permeated with Mary's presence. Further, each Saturday in the Roman rite is devoted to Mary. And on the calendar there are a host of Marian feasts.[84] Some of these Marian feasts are theological in origin. For instance, it was at the Council of Ephesus in the fourth century, while hammering out the fine points of doctrine about how Christ's human and divine natures were united, that Mary was declared not only the Mother of Jesus but also the Mother of God. And the Immaculate Conception and the Assumption have in the last several centuries been deemed official teachings by the Roman pontiffs. Many of the other feasts are more devotional in origin: The appearance of Mary at Lourdes for instance or the stories of the birth of Mary, which derive from very early gospel narratives that circulated among Christians but were not accepted into the official canon of scripture. Still others mark events that are recorded in the canon of scripture. It is these last Marian feasts that all the denominations in some way share.

In Catholic tradition, Marian days are set aside. So too are Marian months. Although the post-Vatican II Catholic Church has downplayed Mary as a prominent figure, in many quarters the months of May and October are still dedicated to her. May processions that culminate in a crown of flowers being placed upon a statue of Our Lady are still organized in parochial schools. And schoolchildren still learn the rosary by praying it daily during the month of October.

It is the rosary, interestingly enough, that in my experience has captured the fancy of many Protestants seeking for new (to them) Christian, embodied, and richly evocative ways to pray. A rosary is, of course, a circle of prayer beads strung at intervals along a chain. Traditionally, as one fingers the beads, one recites the ancient Marian prayer,

> *Hail Mary, full of grace,*
> *the Lord is with you!*
> *Blessed are you among women!*
> *and blessed is the fruit of your womb, Jesus.*
> *Holy Mary, mother of God,*
> *pray for us sinners,*
> *now and at the hour of our death. Amen.*

The Hail Mary beads are interspersed with beads that call for trinitarian prayers or the Lord's Prayer. The roots of Marian devotion stretch far back in Christian history but the rosary came to the fore in the fifteenth century when it was popularized by the Dominican order of preachers. As one prays the fifteen "decades" of prayer beads, one is counseled to focus attention on the great "mysteries" of Mary's life, mysteries that are intertwined with the mystery of her Son. There are three sets of mysteries—"Joyful," "Sorrowful" and "Glorious"—each of which celebrate five events that provide windows into which the human heart can gaze upon Mary's heart as she with motherly love accompanies her child in his earthly and heavenly itinerary.[85]

The rosary is a repetitive, embodied form of prayer. The beads are fingered rhythmically and the prayers recited almost by rote. Ritual specialists will point out that such rhythmic, repetitious prayer has the capacity to carry the devotee into a state of awareness that frees him or her from the tyranny of the overly analytic mind, allowing for a peace-filled, more intuitive, and holistic grasp of reality. Rote, repetitious prayers can be potentially deadening to the spirit, but they also have the capacity to be liberating and healing.

I have always loved the whole panoply of Marian images and observances, a fact about which I am often self-conscious when in the company of ardent Catholic women seeking to reform the church who grew up with an oppressive image of Mary as the eternal good Catholic school girl who never questions Father and keeps her lowly place. That is hardly the whole Mary, either in her biblical manifestation or in her guises as Queen of Saints and Angels, Holy Mother of God, Second Eve, Bride of God, Ladder Spanning Heaven and Earth, Throne of Wisdom, Intercessor, and tender mother of all the faithful. The sheer number of prayers, petitions, hymns, and devotional imagery with Mary at their center that have flowed from the hearts of Christians is unimaginable. Their beauty is often unsurpassed, as is the eloquence of this prayer that tradition attributes to Thomas à Kempis, fourteenth-century author of the *Imitation of Christ*.

Hail, Mary, full of grace, the Lord is with thee. Hail, hope of the needy, Mother of those who no longer possess a mother. O Mary, when my broken heart moans and is filled with sorrow, when my soul is enveloped in sadness and fear, when the wind of temptation blows, when stormy passions break loose in my soul, when my sins have closed the gates of heaven against me and robbed me of the friendship of my God, in this hour of tribulation and anguish, to whom should I have recourse but to thee, O Blessed Mary, consoler of the afflicted and refuge of sinners?

O Mary, thou art indeed that beautiful star of the sea, who saves all those who in the hour of danger raise their eyes to you. I cry to you, then, for help this day, O most merciful Mother of God! I fly to thee with the confidence with which little children take refuge in their mother's arms. Open thine to me: give me the right to take shelter in thy heart; let me hear from your lips the sweet words: "Fear nothing, I am your advocate, I will plead for you: as a mother consoles her weeping child, I will console you." My Mother, say these words, and peace will return to my heart. Come, O Mary, come, with thy constant sweetness, to visit me in my sorrow. Come to raise my courage, to bring me the grace of Jesus. May thy name, full of grace, be, with the adored name of Jesus, the last name I pronounce on earth.[86]

★   ★   ★

On occasion, among the many catalogues that appear unbidden in our home mailbox, we will receive a catalogue from a company that specializes in products for the well-to-do, contemporary spiritual seeker. These are not the catalogues of church products for religious educators or the fruitcakes and Christmas card advertisements from monastic communities or the inspirational books and tapes available from all quarters of the Christian community, be they evangelical, fundamentalist, conservative Catholic, liberal Catholic, or mainstream Protestant. These are nondenominational, not faith-specific goods for the modern American spiritual seeker. Generally the goods seem very expensive, (but then all the commercial catalogues that circulate amaze me for I cannot fathom a consuming public that can or would spend the dollars requested for knickknacks, bric-a-brac, and nonfunctional, noneducational goods that are routinely offered for sale). The spiritual seeker advertisements make available a full spectrum of tapes, books, and implements to soothe, calm, and center the devotee. There are slant boards for head-down relaxation, Tibetan temple bells, oils for aromatherapy, prayer rugs inspired by the Islamic tradition, recorded wolf, ocean, and porpoise sounds, and yoga instruction booklets. Each of these products is a fine thing in and by itself. It is the cumulative reading of the catalog that always astounds one, for the assumption that underlies the list of goods is that spirituality is to be equated with a calm, stress-free state of being. Perhaps this is unfair, but it also tends to give the impression that spiritual awareness is something that one can buy or at least obtain through the use of products. (But that is less a commentary on these particular products than a commentary on our entire culture in which everything—identity, beauty, knowledge, meaning, love—is marketed as a product that can be bought and sold.)

A certain inner peace or equilibrium may well be considered a component of the spiritual life, and it is true that phrases like "detachment" or "the peace that passes all understanding" or "abandonment to divine providence" dot the tradition. But I have the impression that spiritual seekers today are sometimes looking more for stress reduction and personal enhancement than to be aligned with the movement of the Spirit in the world. And I think this is true of Christian seekers as well as people outside or on the margins of Christianity. Sometimes this assumed spiritual well-being takes the form of a constant spiritual "high." There are periods of great intensity and dynamism in the spiritual life and there are forms of religious expression—for example charismatic or pentecostal—that encourage and continue to foster intense affectivity and emotional fervor. But in general, the spiritual life, at least as classically conceived, exhibits a good deal more variation. One can get stuck thinking that the flush of excitement that comes with a new practice or type of prayer is the experience of God. As with any long-term relationship, one needs to stick it out through the times of difficulty or dryness to move into a deeper and more meaningful phase of relating.

Classically, the Christian spiritual life has been envisioned as having three major phases: the purgative, the illuminative, and the unitive. Now, anything as fluid and personalized as an individual's spiritual life cannot be neatly fit into predetermined categories. Nevertheless, there is value in this threefold categorization for it does acknowledge the fact that there are rhythms and seasons in our spirituality just as in other facets of our lives. Basically, the categories describe the letting go we have to do to begin to center our lives on God (purgation), the growing consciousness of God's grace drawing us nearer (illumination) and, finally, the conjoining of our lives with God (union). This characterization oversimplifies things, for the phases are not always clearly separated and each may be varied itself. Further, the three-fold path is often used to describe a mystical ascent that is outside the experience of most people. Regardless of that, the very idea that the journey with and into God requires more than simply feeling good or feeling calm and peaceful is instructive. The Christian tradition (and all other major traditions for that matter) stress that the spiritual journey is a process of being unmade and remade. That process often includes feelings of peace, rejoicing, gratitude, and release, but it includes much more.

It has been my own experience, and I have witnessed this in many others, that an intentional spiritual journey often begins with a period of intense consolation. Feelings of having come home, discovering a treasure, falling in love, being accompanied, drawn out or toward something by an irresistible force. The journey may have been precipitated by some disruption of ordinary life like a divorce, death, failure, illness, or disillusionment. In this period of wondrous warmth and discovery the journeyer is very aware of the presence of God. It may be a much more immediate sensibility than was ever available to the person before. The world seems full of signs and wonders, happy "coincidences" easily occur, dreams, songs, images, personal encounters all seem charged with spiritual meaning. This intense phase may go on for a long time. It may even out last some. It may recur periodically. The journey some people enjoy is basically of this type.

But there are other dynamics of the spiritual journey as well. Persons who have established a relationship with God and kept faithful to it may quite inexplicably find themselves bereft of God's presence. The experience falls under the classic category of "dark night of the soul." The term dark night is not best used to describe depression or bereavement (although these may run parallel to a dark-night experience) or to describe the emptiness or absence persons may feel when they have no relation or only a superficial relation to God. The dark night referred to here is the felt sense of God's absence in a person who has been deeply aware of and attentive to divine presence for a considerable time. Dark nights may be triggered by some unbidden catastrophe or they may simply emerge in the midst of what seems an uninterrupted life. Their main characteristic is that one's most intimate experience of God disappears. There is only darkness, meaninglessness, emptiness and fear. The prayers, the language, the imagery, the relationships, the ideas, the consolations we have relied on to mediate God's presence have vanished.

Virtually everyone on a spiritual path has some similar experience. For many people these times are brief. They often signal a profound transition. Sometimes the experience of dark night is long-lived. On occasion it may become a person's habitual pathway. Any dark night, of whatever duration or intensity, is usually a sign of a deep inward "repatterning" that is taking place. The journeyer is being transformed and inaugurated into a life truly centered on God.

Darkness and emptiness are not particularly pleasant places to be. But it is essential in a genuine dark-night experience (as distinguished from clinical depression) not to run away. For the darkness is its own best teacher. There we become aware of the ways in which our "false" selves, the selves constructed by appearances, power, and possessions, must give way. There too we discover the "god" of our false selves. We had relied on this "god" to give us what we needed to keep up appearances, have power and possessions. This "god" needs to die along with our false selves. The entire process is wildly unfamiliar. We are like blind persons in foreign territory, wandering we know not where. Sometimes it is simply the case that the "god" we have come to depend on is too narrow and cramped. This "god" has upheld our petty prejudices or our damaging opinions. It is not that we exchange one god for another but that we are gradually introduced to the width and breadth, depth and height of God who is beyond our imagining. (This is a process that should, rightly, never cease for it is incomprehensible to think that we will ever fully "know" the fullness of God.) Through our experiences of the dark night we begin to "unknow" rather than know in the old ways to which we are accustomed. We begin to let God be God. It is said that as a person prays for years and years, that prayer itself simplifies. Out of the many concerns, arguments, reasonings, and desires that fuel our prayer emerges a contemplative "nonexperience," a standing stripped of all our powers in awe before the immensity of we know not what. When we are forced beyond the usual analytical levels of knowing because we have exhausted the possibilities found there, we move to unknowing. In this empty place, we may meet God.[87]

Much discernment and the companionship of wise and experienced mentors is necessary to anyone encountering a dark night. The Christian spiritual tradition teaches us that to find ourselves we must transcend ourselves. Our growth in God is not only or always a process of accumulating more spiritual "highs"—be they visions, dreams, a sense of vivid presence, consolations, or whatever. It is as much a process of letting go, being unmade and undone, repatterned in a fashion we could never have imagined, led into the arms of a God whose voice is silence and whose name we can never know.

A decade ago, when we were living in Boston, I made the acquaintance of an affable, middle-aged Jesuit priest who was engaged in ministry in the inner city. During our Boston sojourn this priest was diagnosed with cancer of a sort that has a very poor prognosis for recovery. He quite swiftly became inactive and while undergoing chemotherapy was confined to a convalescent facility. There, he found himself waking every night around 3 A.M. Having previously heard me sing, he contacted me and asked if I would tape-record several songs that he loved as well as read aloud the Johannine scripture passage of the raising of Lazarus from the dead. I did and he used the tapes as meditation material during his nocturnal prayers. I cannot say that I know in much detail the shape of this priest's experience of God, but I am aware that it became luminous, that as he was obliged to unmake, rethink, and wrestle with the meaning of his life and abandon his previously held notions of what God asked of him and how God was involved in his life, he came to a deep and luminous apprehension. When I visited him in the facility, briefly because his energy was so limited, he gave me one of the laminated cards he had requested be made up. On the front was a photograph of a field of dazzling yellow and purple crocus. On

the reverse was a poem composed in God's voice that proclaimed, "I am who am."

The evening of life, like the evening of the day, is a blessed
time of spaciousness, of expanded vision, gentleness, and rest. A
time in which daytime ways of being are done and new ways of
being discovered. A time of letting go, of releasing and relin-
quishing. The prayers of such times rise with a sweet fragrance
like no other.

Alpha and Omega

(Early November)

Children of the heav'n-ly Father
Safely in his bosom gather;
Nestling bird or star in heaven
Such a refuge ne'er was given.

God his own doth tend and nourish,
In his holy courts they flourish.
From all evil things he spares them,
In his mighty arms he bears them.

Neither life nor death shall ever
From the Lord his children sever;
Unto them his grace he showeth,
And their sorrows all he knoweth.

Though he giveth or he taketh,
God his children ne'er forsaketh;
His the loving purpose solely
To preserve them pure and holy.[88]

IN THE FOG-SHROUDED FORESTS OF BAVARIA, HILDEGARD OF BIN-
gen, a twelfth-century Benedictine abbess, poet, and musician,
gave her life to the cultivation of intimacy with God. When she
was approximately forty years old, and after decades of debilitating
illness, Abbess Hildegard revealed the visions that were the source
of the pain plaguing her since childhood. Her *Scivias*, which she
narrated to a scribe, was an extraordinary tapestry of cosmic scope
that ranged from the creation of the world through the fall and re-

demption of humankind, denounced the world's vices and hurled enigmatic prophecies of disaster. At the close of her visionary epic Hildegard envisioned the symphony of the blessed: the angels, patriarchs, prophets, apostles, and the martyred, confessing and virgin saints. They were the ones who would preside over the end of the world. She sang of them in lustrous prose.

Then I saw the lucent sky, in which I heard different kinds of music, marvelously embodying all the meanings I had heard before. I heard the praises of the joyous citizens of Heaven . . .

And their song, like the voice of a multitude, making music in harmony praising the ranks of Heaven, had these words:

. . . .

To the martyrs

. . . .

O rose blossoms, blessed in the joy of your blood's effusion!
Your fragrant blood flowed from the inner counsel
Of Him Who has been always, without beginning,
And planned before time began His great redemption.
*   Your company is honor, whose blood abounded*
To build the Church in the stream from your noble wounds.

And another song sung:

To the confessors

. . . .

*   O ye who imitate the Most Exalted,*
In His most precious and glorious Sacrament!

How great is your glory, in which the power is given
To loose and bind the indolent and the straying,
To beautify white and black, and lift their burdens.
  Yours too is the office of the angelic order,
And yours is the task of knowing the firm foundations
And where to lay them; and therefore great is your honor.

And another song resounded:

To the virgins

  O noble verdure, which grows from the Sun of splendor!
Your clear serenity shines in the Wheel of Godhead,
Your greatness is past all earthly understanding,
And Heavn's wonders surround you in their embrace.
  You glow like dawn, and burn like the Sun in glory.[89]

At the close of the liturgical year the church celebrates last things—the end of life and the end of time. Mysteriously and wondrously, it approaches these endings as beginnings—the beginning of eternal life and the beginning of God's time. This is a season of closures and of the new moment born as closures eclipse the moment that is passing away. It is also a season that celebrates the fullness and fruition of all things, a season that plumbs the depths of human longing to realize the beauty, joy, and completion we sense latent in our lives.

Inaugurating the month of last things is the great solemnity, All Saints, observed on November 1 with the shining white of liturgical garments. The official Christian celebration of the saints has roots in the ninth century and is built upon even more ancient Celtic observances of the autumnal dying and memorials for the dead. Christians, of course, had been honoring their dead long before the ninth century. They had intuited that certain very special dead, the martyrs, held a privileged place in the community. The martyrs were the holy ones, the ones who in their own bodies participated in the crucified and resurrected life of the victorious Christ. The martyrs existed at a sacred cross-roads between heaven and earth, acting as bridges between the two realms, realms separated before the great boundary-breaking event of the Resurrection. The early church taught that the martyrs went directly to the side of God and could intercede there on behalf of the living. Moreover, the power of the resurrected life was available to the community at the sites where the martyrs' remains were entombed. Their graves became the focal point of the church's worship and believers sought healing there. They were the saints.

When martyrdom was no longer an ever-present possibility for Christians, the church held up other special members to be remembered as the martyrs were. Healers, miracle workers, ascetics, ecclesial leaders, persons of heroic virtue, apologists, and theologians all became noted as saints. By the ninth century the church had set aside a feast for all of them.

The saints were sung and celebrated. The liturgical calendar, that rhythmic and cyclical recapitulation of the birth, life, death, and resurrection of Jesus Christ, filled out with memorials honoring the saints. Hymns, legends, prayers, and images extolling their lives and powers abounded.

The sense that the saints were exemplary and that they could act as conduits for divine power emerged quite early. But Saint Paul had not conceived of the saints in quite that way. He saw the church, the body of Christ, as an organic unity whose holiness flowed from Christ through baptism. The saints were all the body's members sanctified through incorporation. This sense of the saints still endures today in Christianity sometimes as official theology, sometimes simply as a felt sensibility. It is not uncommon for Christians to honor the "ordinary saints"—parents, grandparents, mentors, friends—whose lives have consisted of small acts of love and goodness, as well as those whose actions have been heroic. But however the word *saint* is defined, on All Saints the Christian communion worldwide turns attention to the "holy ones."

Those holy ones are as varied as the eras and places from which they come. On the Roman calendar are November memorials of a cluster of specific saints.

November 4	Charles Borromeo
November 11	Martin of Tours
November 12	Josaphat
November 13	Frances Xavier Cabrini
November 15	Albert the Great
November 16	Margaret of Scotland and Gertrude the Great
November 22	Cecilia
November 23	Clement and Columba
November 30	Andrew

Together they represent the wide spectrum of persons deemed suitable exemplars and intercessors by the one denomination that officially canonizes its saints.

This specific cloud of witnesses remembered in November runs the gamut: an aristocratic Counter Reformation Italian Archbishop who founded seminaries and the Confraternity of Christian Doctrine for the education of children and was zealous in his charity for plague victims; a fourth-century ex-soldier convert became a bishop of France, a patron of monasticism, remembered for his wonderworking as well as his peacemaking; an early twentieth-century Italian nun turned-American-citizen, the foundress of the Missionary Sisters of the Sacred Heart who worked among and on behalf of poor immigrants; a medieval scholastic theologian; an eleventh-century Scottish queen fabled for her piety and charity to the poor; a thirteenth-century German abbess, a visionary and mystic authoress; a young martyr venerated in the catacombs of the early Roman church, later honored as the patron saint of church music; a first-century

martyred Roman pope remembered for the pastoral letters that
helped shape the formation of church life; a sixth-century Irish
missionary who brought Celtic monasticism to the continent;
one of the twelve apostles, brother of Peter.

The variety of these witnesses is overwhelming. But it pales in
comparison with the variety of persons, lifestyles, and actions that
Christians have deemed holy over the years. While great and
heroic personages such as these may inspire us to stretch the narrow boundaries of our little lives to respond more generously to
God's invitation to enter the kingdom, we are also mindful of the
small, hidden ways the kingdom comes to be.

For years when my children were in preschool, kindergarten,
and grade school they routinely brought home pale-blue mimeo-
graphed worksheets at the beginning of each November. They
may have drawn a stick-figure version of their patron saint or
written a brief report on their holy namesake. But always they
were asked to describe a saint they had known. Sometimes it was
Mom, Dad, a grandparent, or a kind relative or friend. Always it
was someone who had reached out in compassion, had tenderly
cared for, listened to, been patient with, or helped them. As
adults, the discernment of what the Christian life calls for is often
complex, the interpretation of what is a loving response not always clear. But we are assured that there are qualities of heart and
mind that issue in actions that incarnate love of God and love of
one another.

It is customary to proclaim the Word from the Gospel of
Matthew on the solemnity of All Saints. We return again to the
reading we heard early in Ordinary Time, the Beatitudes.

Blessed are the poor in spirit, for theirs is the kingdom of heaven.
Blessed are they who mourn, for they will be comforted.
Blessed are the meek, for they will inherit the earth.
Blessed are those who hunger and thirst for righteousness, for they
    will be filled.

Blessed are the merciful, for they will be receive mercy.
Blessed are the pure in heart, for they will see God.
Blessed are the peacemakers, for they will be called children of God.
Blessed are those who are persecuted for righteousness' sake, for theirs
    is the kingdom of heaven.
Blessed are you when people revile you and persecute you and utter
    all kinds of evil against you falsely on my account. Rejoice and
    be glad, for your reward is great in heaven, for in the same way
    they persecuted the prophets who were before you.

(MATTHEW 5:3-12)

They ring in our ears—qualities of the kingdom, the virtues of the transformed life. Each one is an ocean in itself, a vast, unfathomable reservoir of meaning waiting to unfold in myriad ways in the lives of women and men in each new era: the inexhaustible streams of life flowing from the one source of holiness itself, Christ.

★ ★ ★

Years ago I attended a lecture given by a graduate school mentor of mine on the religious thought of the Danish philosopher Søren Kierkegaard. Kierkegaard, he said, wrote a commentary on the biblical injunction, "In all things give thanks." Such an injunction, the philosopher insisted, was essential not because life events naturally elicit from us a spirit of thanks, but because the act of giving thanks was in and of itself formative. It changes things.

At the closure of the church year we are given the opportunity to take stock. We look backward: at the year, at our lives, at our deep shared history as Christians. And we look forward: to next year, to the next life, to the future hope of fulfillment that weaves together the threads of our separate lives. And we are invited to give thanks. The act of thanksgiving presses the sweet nectar of joy from the husks and hulls of everyday life. We harvest the fruits that wait, heavy and ripe, to fall: the thousand small gestures of caring, the struggles with our shortcomings, the legacy of our faithfulness, the lessons learned from disappointments and failure. All of it, gathered up in gratitude.

Americans bring a special focus to the spiritual arts of gratitude because we pause as a nation at harvesttime and give thanks. We decorate our sanctuaries with autumn oranges, yellows, and browns. Sheaves of harvested wheat, pumpkins, nuts, checkered ears of ornamental corn, these are the joyful symbols of work well done, bounty received, the gracious fecundity of God's good earth. How utterly fitting it is at this time of endings to give thanks. For gratitude plucks the ripe fruit from the trees of our spiritual lives so that we might be nourished and fed and we might offer back, in some small measure, a gift for the gifts we have received.

Now thank we all our God
With hearts and hands and voices,
Who wondrous things has done,
In whom his world rejoices;
Who, from our mothers' arms,
Hath blessed us on our way
With countless gifts of love,
And still is ours today.

O may this gracious God
Through all our life be near us,
With ever joyful hearts
And blessed peace to cheer us;
Preserve us in his grace,
And guide us in distress,
And free us from all sin,
Till heaven we possess.[90]

I love as well the end-of-the-year customs found in parts of the United States saturated with Mexican culture. In these regions festivities for the November 1 and 2 observances of All Saints and All Souls, or "Day of the Dead" (El Dia de los Muentos) are elaborate. Families gather at the gravesides of their departed, festooning the sites with paper flowers, picnicking, playing, acknowledging the unbroken communion of love and presence with those who have gone before. Indeed, in small villages, the entire population turns out. Many families decorate *of-frendas* or altars in their homes with candied fruits, sweetbreads, tamales, fruit, mole, and tortillas. They cover them with yellow-orange, marigoldlike flowers, leaving a carpet of petals from their houses to the graves as a guide for their loved ones to follow. Bonfires light the way at night. And Mexican folk art would not be its distinctive self without the striking papier mâché or wooden figures created for the festivals of the dead—those delightful, comedic, chalk-white figurines painted as bold black skeletons: bones dancing, playing fiddle and guitar, grimacing under broad-brimmed sombreros, flouncing their wide skirts. Fiesta breaks through the barriers of life and death, swallows past and future into an eternal, joyful present where we gratefully know ourselves as one communion in the eyes and heart of God.

★   ★   ★

During the last month of the church year, as we celebrate the fullness of last things, we draw inspiration from the strange and wondrous scriptural evocation of the last times. The Apocalypse (The Revelation to John) that closes the canon of the Bible provides us with a wealth of colorful imagery with which to image the completion of all things. The book has frequently served as a template for speculation about historical events leading up to the end of time as we know it. It was, of course, written in the literary genre of apocalyptic, a form common in the era of the church's formation. Its imagery was drawn from contemporary astrological lore. And it has excited past and present speculation about catastrophic end-time scenarios. A more measured approach might help us to see Revelation as a tapestry of ancient and evocative symbols that have resonated through the centuries that still give shape to our deepest hopes and expectations—the realization of a new heaven and earth where God, as Love, reigns.

The supposed author, John, exiled on the island of Patmos, is "caught up in the Spirit." Before him unfolds a mighty cosmic drama: One like the Son of Man declares he is the "First and the Last" and commands John to write. He does. He writes of a heavenly throne surrounded by elders, torches and spirits, of a scroll with seven seals that must be broken, of the horsemen of death, plague, war and famine, of the end times, earthquakes, blood, catastrophes, of a woman clothed with the sun forced to hide her child, of war between a dragon and the Archangel Michael, of beasts and conflict, of the vision of Mount Zion with the Lamb and the 144,000 robed in white singing a new song, the thousand-year reign of Christ.

I saw another angel ascending from the rising of the sun, having the seal of the living God, and he called with a loud voice to the four angels who had been given power to damage earth and sea, saying, "Do not damage the earth or the sea or the trees, until we marked the servants of our God with a seal on their foreheads."

And I heard the number of those who were sealed, one hundred and forty-four thousand, sealed out of every tribe of the people of Israel.

After this I looked, and there was a great multitude that no one could count, from every nation, from all tribes and peoples and languages, standing before the throne and before the Lamb, robed in white, with palm branches in their hands. They cried out in a loud voice, saying,

"Salvation belongs to our God,
who is seated on the
throne, and to the Lamb!"

(REVELATION 7:2-4, 9-12)

All the angels stood around the throne and around the elders and the four living creatures, and they fell on their faces before the throne and worshiped God, singing,

"Amen, Blessing and glory, wisdom
and thanksgiving honor
and power and might
be to our God forever and ever! Amen."

Then one of the elders addressed me, saying, "Who are these, robed in white, and where have they come from?" I said to him, "Sir, you are the one that knows." Then he said to me, "These are they who have come out of the great ordeal; they have washed their robes and made them white in the blood of the Lamb.

For this reason they are before the throne of God,
    and worship him day and night within his temple,
    and the one who is seated on the throne will shelter them.
They will not hunger and thirst no more;
    the sun will not strike them,
    nor any scorching heat;
for the Lamb at the center of the throne will be their shepherd,
    and he will guide them to springs of the water of life,
and God will wipe away every tear from their eyes."

(REVELATION 7:12-17)

This is followed by the unloosing of Satan and the judgment of the dead. Out of these blood-soaked, violent upheavals the

New Jerusalem emerges. Like a bride she comes. God dwelling among humankind. "Behold! I make all things new!" "I am the Alpha and the Omega."

The new Jerusalem. The idea of all cities, jewel-like in splendor, radiant with the divine Glory within her walls, the river with the waters of life, the fecundity of the tree of life. There God is seen face-to-face.

★   ★   ★

The flight from Los Angeles to Omaha, with a layover in St. Louis, was a long one. It gave me ample time to absorb the events of the previous two days. I had retraced my itinerary of twenty-three years before, following the same highway I had traveled when I left the City of the Angels to enroll in graduate school in Santa Barbara where I then resided for ten years. When you have lived in a city for a decade, even if you have been away for years, a return has the effect of collapsing time as you feel your way intuitively around familiar streets, parks, and landmarks. On this return I had stood on the steps of the Old Mission, the same steps where I had stood more than two decades previously with my religious studies professor. We had been on a tour of the Mission as a field trip in his course entitled "From Augustine to Luther." The pastor had led the class on a spiritual pilgrimage through the Francescan life—mixed, part contemplation, part action—and my professor and I had lingered on the top steps as the rest of the class filtered away and gazed out across Saint Barbara's namesake city to the low-lying fog that hung over the Pacific coast. "I feel like I belong here," I said. He nodded saying, "Yes, I do too."

These last two days the fog had burned off and the azure Pacific was vivid and bright. The large crowd was again filtering away from the mission steps, this time following the funeral service that had honored the memory of that same professor, my friend. These two days had been electric with swift returning memories of my graduate school decade, years in which my professor became my dissertation director, my spiritual companion, my children's godfather, and my friend: the two of us exulting in my graduate assistant's office over my first published article; buying apricot bonbons on a lark after a tedious colloquium; nauseous with morning sickness, eating mashed potatoes in a suburban coffee shop as he compensated in joy for the upcoming happy event I was having difficulty appreciating; whispering "Good night" as we padded noiselessly to our respective cells during a class visit to a Trappist monastery; flipping through the Lutheran hymnbook and pouncing upon the perfect hymn for the day, he playing, I singing; laboring over the footnotes for our book; him pacing the hospital halls and comforting my husband while I agonized in labor; finding a red rose on my doorstep after my dissertation defense; flinging ideas for a team-taught course across the garden pathway as I pushed my toddler's stroller and he jogged by on his afternoon exercise; joking in the university parking lot, weekday late afternoon, "Let's blow this fire trap. Let's go to Buellton!" Buellton, a small community a number of miles north of Santa Barbara, was the home of Anderson's Split Pea Soup. Billboards lining the road to the town advertise a cartoon Laurel and Hardy pair named "Split Pea" and "Hap-pea" stirring a huge cauldron of green sludge. Buellton has become a cypher for the endtimes. "When we get to Buellton," we joked. "Next year in Buellton," we promised, echoing the Jewish Passover promise of reunion in Jerusalem.

The memories spill one over the other as familiar sites pass by. Another decade has intervened since I resided in Santa Barbara, but my professor-friend and I never lost touch. Letters, phone calls, e-mail, and visits snatched between our respective busy schedules cemented our bond. It was especially at the annual meeting of the American Academy of Religion that we hoped to connect. The reunions were always different—a few times they could never take place, one or the other of us not attending that year. Breakfast in a Chicago kosher deli, a late-afternoon drive through the Mendocino wine country; a repeated round trip ride on the New Orleans ferry that carried restaurant and hotel employees out of the tourist district. The reunions were a chance to touch base, to laugh, to catch up. Always they were rooted in what had originally brought us together—the common search, pursued through the discipline of religious studies, for the deep life, for the transparency of a life lived open to the presence of God.

Philadelphia was the site of one of our most wonderful reunions. About a month before the annual meeting, my mentor had sent a wry and witty note, which began, "Would Dr. Wright grace us with the pleasure of her company at an outing to the New Jerusalem?" About an hour outside the City of Brotherly Love is the international headquarters of the Swedenborgian Society. A seminary, cathedral, library archives, and extensive museum make up the compound. The Society, knowing the Academy was to meet in Philadelphia, had invited a select group of religion scholars to an evening's outing, including dinner and a guided tour of the entire establishment. They wished scholars in the fields of alternative religions or the phenomenology of religion to become familiar with research opportunities available to them. Shall we take a bus ride and have dinner with the Swedenborgians this time? It seemed too delightful a lark to resist.

I did a little homework before I went. Emanuel Swedenborg was an early-eighteenth-century scientist who had spent a lifetime working at the Sweden government's Board of Mines. He was also an incredibly creative intellect, having anticipated in his scientific inquiries, nebular theory, magnetic theory, and the aeroplane. His inventions were many. Swedenborg's inquiring mind had a mystical bent to it as well. He was the son of a Luthern bishop who was also a professor of theology and scripture at Uppsala University and a sense of the spiritual dimension of things compelled him. He attempted to show by scientific analysis that the universe had a fundamental spiritual structure. In midlife he experienced what he described as the direct consciousness of angels and the spiritual realm in normal life and felt commissioned to make his ideals known. Out of this came the idea of the New Church, a spiritual fraternity of all those of various ecclesial allegiances who accepted his doctrines. Central to Swedenborg's vision was the belief in the intimate correspondence between the physical and spiritual worlds. In what is perhaps his greatest work, *The Apocalypse Revealed*, the Swedish mystic plumbed the scriptures to cull out a unique spiritual vision of their inner meaning. He rejected the doctrine of the Trinity; instead, he avowed that God is one in three principles (love, divine wisdom, divine energy), each manifest in Jesus Christ. The New Jerusalem is symbolic of the ideal human society and will become manifest as all human beings accept and practice the spiritual truths revealed in scripture. When this occurs, Jesus will make his second coming in Spirit, not in person.

Saturday night of the Annual Meeting we met with the other select scholars and our tour guides and boarded a chartered van for the ride out to the Swedenborgian headquarters. A number in the group were of Scandinavian origin and my mentor, in typical fashion, got us singing the old hymns from the Lutheran hymnal: songs of longing for home, for the completion of all things.

The evening turned out to be an utterly magical one. The Swedenborgian headquarters was nestled in a Pennsylvania valley settled exclusively by society members a century before. Hills cupped the community of the New Jerusalem, verdant lawns flocked with late autumn-leafed trees swept between members' homes. Nestled in the cup's bottom was the magnificent Cathedral of Bryn Athyn, a huge, northern-European Gothic structure constructed according to the spiritual architectural principles of Emanuel Swedenborg. Bryn Athyn contains no straight lines for the mystic scientist had observed that nature, which is revelatory of spirit, has no straight lines. Only natural materials had been used, dark hardwood and gleaming granite especially. All the walls were slightly convex and the Cathedral floor elevated a total of almost a foot from the front doors to the altar. Everything was exquisitely hand carved with vegetative designs. And the place was saturated in symbols from the Revelation to John. Around the altar loomed seven golden candlesticks, the ambo was carved all around with jewel-like imagery of the city-bride and the Lamb's banquet, stained glass shimmered with depictions of the promised new earth.

Our guide led us from the Cathedral to the seminary library where the Swedenborg archives are housed. There the mystic scientist's astonishing mind revealed itself, his painstaking observations and calculations of the physical universe having yielded affirmations of the spiritual substructure sustaining and shaping all that is. Finally, we were escorted to a nearby Scottish baronial castle, former home of a Society member who had made his fortune in the last century in plate glass. Formerly the residence for a bustling family, the castle had been deeded to the Society and kept as headquarters and museum for the vast collection of ancient treasures the plate-glass baron had collected over the years. After a brief, informative lecture by our hosts, we dined in the compendious anteroom of the castle whose massive stone walls were hung with medieval tapestries. Then we toured the upper chambers, home to Assyrian friezes, Greek statuary, Roman pottery, Egyptian artifacts and the lower chambers, display room for a breathtaking collection of medieval European stained glass. My mentor-friend and I were swept up in the numinousness of it all: the dark, star-canopied valley, the glittering vision of the New Jerusalem nestled peacefully among the hills, the strange magical antiquity of this turreted Scottish castle cropping up. Our tour took us to an upper balcony that overlooked the surroundings. The carpet of lights that was Philadelphia winked at us from across a dark distance. We lingered behind our group a bit, savoring the evening's stillness, then crept back into the cornucopia of castle rooms, finding ourselves finally in a small round music conservatory just large enough for a foot-pumped organ and a few chairs. Several Swedenborgian hymnals lay about and, letting our tour group move ahead of us once more, my mentor and I flipped through the pages. "Shall we?" he queried sitting down at the keyboard.

"Yes," I readily replied. And we found a familiar melody, with lyrics somewhat altered to reflect the Society's theological perspective, and he began to play as I sang.

As we emerged from the conservatory a fellow visitor stuck his head through the doorway. "I can't believe it. Where was that coming from? I thought I heard angels singing," he breathed. We smiled, for we knew in some strange way what he thought was true.

On the bus ride home we gloried together about our strange and wondrous evening, how we had sung our way through the Lutheran hymnbook to the New Jerusalem, and how it shone and with what beauty and how we had felt there the deep springs of our long friendship well up and overflow. The convergence of heaven and earth. Later we would half-joke about the New Jerusalem. But we knew we were really talking about the exquisitely beautiful and powerful longing for God that stretched tight beneath everything we did and were.

It had even come up in an e-mail I sent to him Wednesday, October 22.

Fall has fallen. Sleet and snow today. Heading out of town to Missouri for a pastoral gathering tomorrow. Thinking of you deciding all those things, meeting everyone halfway on everything. It will be different in the New Jerusalem. I trust it will also be equally interesting.

He replied on Thursday, October 28:

Because e-mail was down I just read this message this morning before departing for D.C. Thanks so much for your understanding. Hope Nebraska warms up.

That same evening a mutual friend phoned to inform me that my mentor-friend had collapsed from a heart attack in the Washington Dulles International Airport and died. The funeral was held at the Old Mission in his present and my former hometown. I stood on the steps overlooking the azure Pacific where the two of us had stood twenty-three years before. It had come full circle—to completion. His family had asked me to sing at the service. I was sent a copy of a short hymn he had composed as a young man of eighteen. His music, my voice once more. The date was Monday, November 3, just following All Saints and All Souls.

The music and scripture for the festal days extended themselves into the funeral service. The choir sang:

For all the saints who from their labors rest,
All who by faith before the world confessed,
Your name, O Jesus, be forever blest.
Alleluia! Alleluia!

You were the rock, their fortress and their might;
You, Lord, their Captain in their well-fought fight;
You in the darkness drear, their one true light.
Alleluia! Alleluia!

O may your soldiers, faithful, true and bold,
Fight as the saints who nobly fought of old,
And win with them, the victor's crown of gold.
Alleluia! Alleluia!

O blest communion, family divine!
We feebly struggle, they in glory shine;
Yet all are one within your great design.
Alleluia! Alleluia!

And when the strife is fierce, the warfare long,
Steals on the ear the distant triumph song,
And hearts are brave again, and arms are strong.
Alleluia! Alleluia!

The golden evening brightens in the west;
Soon, soon to faithful warriors comes their rest;
Sweet is the calm of paradise the blest.
Alleluia! Alleluia!

But then there breaks a yet more glorious day:
The saints triumphant rise in bright array;
The King of glory passes on his way.
Alleluia! Alleluia!

From earth's wide bounds, from ocean's farthest coast,
Through gates of pearl streams in the countless host,
Singing to Father, Son, and Holy Ghost:
Alleluia! Alleluia! [91]

And we listened to the reading from the Revelation to John:

Then I saw a new heaven and a new earth; for the first heaven and
earth had passed away, and the sea was no more. And I saw the holy
city, the new Jerusalem, coming down out of heaven from God, pre-
pared as a bride adorned for her husband. And I heard a loud voice
from the throne saying,

*   "See, the home of God is among mortals.*

He will dwell with them as their God;
they will be his peoples,
and God himself will be with them;
he will wipe every tear from their eyes.
Death will be no more;
mourning and crying and pain will be no more.
for the first things have passed away."

And the one who was seated on the throne said, "See, I am mak-
ing all things new." Also he said, "Write this, for these words are
trustworthy and true." Then he said to me, "It is done! I am the
Alpha and Omega, the beginning and the end. To the thirsty I will
give water as a gift from the spring of the water of life.

(REVELATION 21:1-6)

November brings the church year to a close. It is the month in which we celebrate last things: the end of time, the end of life. We celebrate completion and fullness. We lean with longing into the proffered vision of a new heaven and a new earth. We remember with gratitude all the saints, all the souls, whose hearts have been opened wide enough to receive the sweetness of that longing. We remember those who have walked hand in hand with us into the promise that this life, these loves, these longings are the very pathways by which we will, at the completion, come face-to-face with God.

With Me, before Me, behind Me

(Last Week of Ordinary Time)

Christ with me, Christ before me, Christ behind me,
Christ in me, Christ beneath me, Christ above me,
Christ on my right, Christ on my left,
Christ when I lie down, Christ when I sit down, Christ when I arise,
Christ in the heart of everyone who speaks of me,
Christ in the eye that sees me,
Christ in the ear that hears me.[92]

I HAD WALKED IN THE CHILL NOVEMBER AIR THE TEN BLOCKS from the conference hotel, down Stockton, past Market Street, and around the corner to San Francisco's Saint Patrick's Church humming fragments of the hymn,

> *Ride on, Jesus, ride.*
> *Ride on, Jesus, ride. . . .*
>
> *King Jesus rides on a milk white horse.*
> *. . . The river Jordan he did cross.*
>
> *Ride on, Jesus, conquering king . . .*
>
> *. . . my Jesus lifted his throne above,*
> *See his mercy and his love.*
>
> *Ride on, Jesus, ride.*
> *Ride on, Jesus, conquering King*
> *Ride on, Jesus, ride.*[93]

It was the last Sunday of the church year, and we were celebrating the solemnity of Christ the King. Saint Patrick's turned
out to be a fantastic hundred-year-old structure which, as an
inner-city parish, had served a succession of ethnic Catholic pop-
ulations over the years. The present community was predominantly Filipino and apparently partly first generation for the sign
on the confessional door near the side pew into which I slipped
read "English, Tagalog, Cebuano, Hiligaynon and Ilocano." It had
been a full Sunday of conference sessions attended, and I had had
to walk briskly in order to be on time for the 5:15 service. As I
took off my coat and settled down, the visual feast of the interior
came into focus. Ethnic parishes are often rich with the devotional imagination of pre-Vatican II Catholicism, and Saint
Patrick's was no exception. The sanctuary was crowded with
bright, polychromed statuary and votive lights flickered at the
many side altars. Most striking was the pagentry of the service itself for, along with the anticipated priest and altar servers, a pa-
rade of perhaps a dozen white-and-red-robed women and men
processed in to the vigorous chords of "The King of Glory
Comes." These, as it turned out, were the lay eucharistic ministers, uncharacteristically robed and processing. We were led in
full-throated song by a white-robed, middle-aged Filipino ma-
tron and a slightly younger, grey-habited nun who hung back
from the microphone and timidly followed our cantor's vigorous
lead. Saint Patrick's was a different universe from the many communities with which I usually have occasion to worship. Inner-
city, urban, poor, ethnic, only marginally English speaking, it was
a wonderful place to celebrate the solemnity of Christ the King
because there I was acutely aware of the global fellowship of the
followers of Christ.

The final scriptural image that shapes the liturgical year is suggested in part by Book of Revelation: the King of kings and Lord
of lords descends from the opened heavens on a white horse to
strike the nations and tread out in the winepress the wine of the

wrath of God. Here is the King. The Alpha and the Omega. The Beginning and the End.

As an educated, American woman aware of the way religious language and imagery convey implicit ideas and support all sorts of social institutions and practices—not all of which are in sync with the gospel—I cannot claim that the image of Christ as king is always for me a comfortable one. Especially when it is linked to triumphal notions of church or colonial ideologies that seek to dominate. But I can do the image when I join it with other images that refract the Christ-event: Jesus riding a donkey into Jerusalem in a manner that confounds our ideas of kingship, the vulnerability of a child in a manger, the deep self-emptying of the man hanging abandoned on a cross under the sign "King of the Jews." And I can do the image when I consider the human family and our shared life and when I consider the two great commandments that lay the foundation for the teachings of Jesus of Nazareth:

"Love the Lord your God with all your heart, with all your soul, with all your mind." That is the greatest commandment. It comes first. The second is like it: "Love your neighbour as yourself."

(MATTHEW 22: 37-39, NEB)

I hear those great utterances with ears alerted to the rich religious and cultural diversity of today's global village. And I hear them say, "Let love suffuse your life. Let the source of life to which your faith points be at your heart's center. Know you are loved the same way and know each other person as so loved. Know each other as another self." English poet William Blake spoke the mystery so well when he offered that

And are put on earth a little space,
That we may learn to bear the beams of love.[94]

This kind of knowledge is not easily come by, this loving not easily achieved. We begin to know and love this way when we allow our narrow, false selves to be decentered, when we discover God as our true identity, when we let Love itself establish a kingdom in our hearts. Christ is the liberating one who points to the reign of Love, the beloved one who teaches us we are each beloved. Through the rhythms and cycles of our lives—the beginnings and endings, the sacramental moments, the intertwining rhythms of daily life and prayer, the years of worship and work, caretaking and tending, the dyings and risings, the textures and tastes of our ordinary existences lived with attention to the mystery of God with us—we anticipate the kingdom.

If I walk in the world on a path hollowed out by generations of persons who too have found their way on the road that wends from Bethlehem to the empty tomb by way of Calvary, I can only think of this road as a royal one. It is like the road I traveled hundreds of times as a girl along the coast of California, El Camino Real, the King's Highway, that coastal highway that was fashioned broad and wide enough for the retinue of the king to pass along it. Our lives are such a road, if only we would know the mystery at their heart.

APPENDICES

I. Guide to Reading
The Time Between

THE LITURGICAL SEASON OF ORDINARY TIME DOES NOT REMAIN stable from year to year. Depending upon the placement of Easter (which hinges on the lunar cycle) and thus of Ash Wednesday, and depending upon the day of the week on which Christmas falls, Ordinary Time may contain either thirty-three or thirty-four Sundays. Further, the first segment of the season, after the Christmas cycle ceases and the Lenten cycle begins, may be quite brief or fairly long. Correspondingly, the extended period from Pentecost until Advent's commencement may range from twenty-two to twenty-eight weeks. The season cannot, however, be conceptualized as a continuous narrative broken by an intermission because several fixed feasts, notably Trinity Sunday and the feasts that follow it, always fall on the Sundays after Pentecost. The changing focus on each of the synoptic Gospels over a period of three years futhers the complexity.

Thus I have struggled to structure a book that can be read in a meditative fashion throughout all three of the cycles of readings and from year to year with the changes in placement that is necessitated. I have decided against a book divided into thirty-three or -four segments to match the Sunday celebrations, although this would make sense from a number of perspectives, chiefly since it would highlight the significance of the ancient weekly feast. But it seemed too rigid and fragmented a structure to allow for the variety found in the season, both in the changing lengths of the season's two parts, the differing vantage points of the three evangelists, and the myriad of saints' days and minor feasts that variously do or do not fall within the perimeters of ordinary time.

I have settled on a two-segment pattern preceded by an introduction entitled "The Season of Ordinary Time." Part 1, "Call and Response," with its five chapters is meant to be read during the post Epiphany and pre-Lenten segment of Ordinary Time.

★ "At Water's Edge" is intended as reading for the first week of the season, a week prefaced by the liturgical celebration of Jesus' baptism in the river Jordan. It considers baptism and our identity as beloved daughters and sons.

★Morning prayer, conversion, and the January 25 feast of Saint Paul's conversion are treated in "A Fresh Beginning."

★"The Lord's Day" invites reflection on the central Christian feast day—Sunday—and introduces Matthew's Gospel, with the Beatitudes, its centerpiece, as a template for discipleship.

★"An Offering" corresponds to the ancient February 2 Feast of the Presentation of the Lord, plays with the imagery of light as a metaphor for discipleship, and considers the relationship of marriage.

★"Good Gifts" is meant to be read in mid- to late-February in the short (in some years) period before Ash Wednesday. It explores family life.

Part 2, "The Way That Lies Before," with its eleven chapters is intended for reflection in the days following Pentecost.

★The "Three-in-One" chapter corresponds to Trinity Sunday, makes note of the feast of the Visitation, and reflects on spiritual friendship.

★The body is the subject of "God's Body": the body of Christ's church, the mystery of God's embodied presence with us, and the earth considered as God's body. It corresponds to the observances on the Roman calendar of the Body and Blood of Christ and, on some Protestant calendars, of Environmental Sunday.

★"Gathered In" is devoted to a discussion of Peter's confession of faith, introduces the Lucan Gospel's model of discipleship, the June 24 solemnity of the birth of John the Baptist and the accounts of the missioning of the disciples.

★The segment entitled "Day by Day" deals with the creation of a rule of life, explores the Rule of Saint Benedict, and introduces Jesus' parables of the kingdom.

★Forgiveness, reconciliation, and the late-July, early-August liturgical celebrations honoring Mary Magdalene and the Transfiguration are the focus of "Much Has Been Forgiven."

★"Is There a Balm?" speaks of healing, introduces Mark's Gospel as a template for discipleship, and considers the arts of spiritual discernment.

★"Lifted Up" focuses upon the mid-September celebration of the triumph of the cross, considers martyrdom as the prototypical form of Christian holiness, and explores the practice of the virtues.

★The late September, early October memorials of the guardian angels and of the archangels, the arts of spiritual companionship, and the ancient practice of the works of mercy form the nucleus of the chapter "Watching over Me."

★"Rising like Incense" introduces the daily observance of evening prayer with its Marian canticle, considers the eventide of life and the experience of dark night.

★"Alpha and Omega" explores the last month of the church year with its celebrations of All Saints, All Souls, and Thanksgiving with their profound harvest images of the end of life and the end of time.

★The final brief chapter, "With Me, Before Me, Behind Me," is meant to be read on the final solemnity of the church year, Christ the King.

The season of Ordinary Time ends, of course, with the beginning of the new church year on the first Sunday of Advent. For readers who wish to follow the narrative week by week, I suggest breaking the chapters down into the smaller sections separated by asterisks and spacing out the readings to fit the division of weeks in a given year. I have constructed them to be fairly lengthy so I trust they will provide enough texture and variance whether they are lingered over or read as intact chapters.

The sources I have relied upon in writing *The Time Between* come from the various churches: United States Catholic Conference, *Liturgy Documentary Series 6, Norms Governing Liturgical Calendars* (Washington, D.C. USCC, 1984); *Lutheran Book of Worship* (Minneapolis: Augsberg Publishers and Board of Publication, Luthern Church in America, Philadelphia; 1978); *The Book of Common Prayer* (According to the use of the Episcopal Church,

1979); *Book of Common Worship*, for The Presbyterian Church (U.S.A.) and The Cumberland Presbyterian Church (Philadelphia, Pa.: Westminster John Knox, 1993); *For All the Saints: A Calendar of Commemorations for United Methodists*, edited by Clifton F. Guthrie (Akron, Ohio: Order of Saint Luke Publishing, 1995).

II. Table of the Liturgical Calendar (1999–2010)

Church Year (A, B, C)	First Sunday of Advent	Epiphany	Ash Wed.	Easter	Pentecost
B/1999–2000	Nov. 28	Jan. 6	March 9	April 23	June 11
C/2000–2001	Dec. 3	Jan. 6	Feb. 28	April 15	June 3
A/2001–2002	Dec. 2	Jan. 6	Feb. 13	March 31	May 19
B/2002–2003	Dec. 1	Jan. 6	March 5	April 20	June 8
C/2003–2004	Nov. 30	Jan. 6	Feb. 25	April 11	May 30
A/2004–2005	Nov. 28	Jan. 6	Feb. 9	March 27	May 15
B/2005–2006	Nov. 27	Jan. 6	March 1	April 16	June 4
C/2006–2007	Dec. 3	Jan. 6	Feb. 2	April 8	May 27
A/2007–2008	Dec. 2	Jan. 6	Feb. 6	March 23	May 11
B/2008–2009	Nov. 30	Jan. 6	Feb. 25	April 12	May 31
C/2009–2010	Nov. 29	Jan. 6	Feb. 17	April 4	May 23

★ In the Roman calendar, Epiphany is placed on the Sunday nearest January 6.

The first segment of the book, "Call and Response," accompanies the season from the Sunday after Epiphany up until Ash Wednesday.

The second segment, "The Way That Lies Before," picks up after Pentecost and continues until the beginning of Advent.

Endnotes

1. *The Vigil: Keeping Watch in the Season of Christ's Coming* (Nashville, Tenn.: Upper Room Books™, 1992) and *The Rising: Living the Mysteries of Lent, Easter and Pentecost* (Nashville, Tenn.: Upper Room Books™, 1994).

2. Christian monasticism developed a more elaborate rhythm of daily prayer that crystallized into the monastic office with its seven "day hours" (lauds, prime, terce, sext, none, vespers, compline) and the "night office" (matins). Each of the monastic hours consists of psalms, hymns, lessons, antiphons, responses and versicles, and prayer. What is today called the office of readings is a more recent innovation in the Divine Office. It replaces the old night office and can be recited any time during the day. Its focus is upon readings from scripture and other devotional literature. Scripture passages for the Office of Readings take their themes from the proceeding Sundays. While the Roman and Anglican-Episcopal churches have been the primary denominations to retain the rhythm of daily liturgical prayer, other denominations have developed worship and prayer resources for both collective and individual daily prayer.

3. From T. S. Eliot, "Four Quartets" in T. S. Eliot: *The Complete Poems and Plays 1909-1950* (New York: Harcourt, Brace and World, 1971), 145.

4. Negro spiritual.

5. Thomas Merton, *Seeds of Contemplation* (Norfolk, Conn.: New Directions Book, 1949), 12-15.

6. Text: Eleanor Farjeon, from "The Children's Bells 1957."

7. These words for the morning liturgy come from *The Upper Room® Worship Book: Music and Liturgies for Spiritual Formation* (Nashville, Tenn.: The Upper Room®, 1985).

8. © David Goodrich 1983. Psalm 63. Text adapted from *Good News Bible* © American Bible Society, 1976.

9. Paul's conversion is celebrated on January 25 in most denominations.

10. S. Chadwick, quoted in James M. Gordon, *Evangelical Spirituality* (London: SPCK, 1991), 312.

11. Whitefield's life is commemorated on the Calendar of Saints for United Methodists on September 30. Cf. *For All Saints: A Calendar of Commemorations for United Methodists*, ed. by Clifton F. Guthrie (Akron, Ohio: Order of Saint Luke Publications, 1995).

12. Quoted in Gordon, 54–55.

13. Ibid., 57.

14. Commemorations for John Wesley and Charles Wesley on the calendar for United Methodists fall on March 2 and 29. *The Book of Common Prayer* remembers them together on March 3, and the *Lutheran Book of Worship* on March 2.

15. John and Charles Wesley, *Selected Writings and Hymns*, ed. by Frank Whaling (New York: Paulist Press, 1981), 176.

16. Ibid., 177–79.

17. Anthony of Egypt's memorial falls on January 17 in the Roman and Methodist calendars and in the *Book of Common Prayer.*

18. Text, Joachim Neander (1650–1680), trans. by Catherine Winkworth, 1827–78, alt.

19. On all the Christian calendars, Matthew's feast is placed on September 21, Mark's on April 25, and Luke's on October 18.

20. The suggestions were given by Donald Senior, C.P. at a 1997 conference in Chicago sponsored by the Sacred Heart Communities in Collaboration. His paper was entitled "Forgiveness From the Heart."

21. *Lutheran Book of Worship* (Minneapolis, Minn.: Augsburg Publishing House and Board of Publication, Lutheran Church in America, 1978). Their commemorations fall on January 13 and 15 in that denomination. The United Methodist calendar places George Fox on January 13, and Martin Luther King Jr. on April 4.

22. Text: Isaiah 6; Dan Schutte, S. J., 1981. Daniel I. Schutte and North American Liturgy Resources.

23. Text, Negro spiritual.

24. Quoted in *For All the Saints*, 82. Harriet Tubman's feast is observed on March 10 on the Commemorative Calendar for United Methodists.

25. "All Good Gifts." Matthias Claudius (1740–1815); trans. Jane Montgomery Campbell (1817–1878).

26. See my *Sacred Dwelling: A Spirituality of Family Life* (Leavenworth,

Kan.: Forest of Peace, 1994) from which part of the above passage is taken.

27. Text: Reginald Heber, 1783-1826, alt.

28. Doxology

29. Augustine's memorial is placed on August 28 on all the Sanctoral calendars.

30. Henri J. M. Nouwen, *Behold the Beauty of the Lord: Praying With Icons* (Notre Dame, Ind.: Ave Maria Press, 1987), 20-21.

31. Jane de Chantal's and Francis de Sales's memorials appear on the Roman calendar on August 21 and January 24.

32. Quoted in Wendy M. Wright, *Bond of Perfection* (New York: Paulist Press, 1985), 103-104.

33. Cf. Wendy M. Wright, *A Retreat With Francis De Sales, Jane De Chantal, and Aelred of Rievaulx: Befriending Each Other in God* (Cincinnati: St. Anthony Messanger Press, 1996).

34. Text: John Marriot, 1780-1825.

35. Text: 1 Corinthians 10:16:17, 12:4, Galatians 3:28; the Didache 9.

36. Gertrude the Great of Helfta, *Spiritual Exercises*, trans. Gertrude J. Lewis and Jack Lewis (Kalamazoo, Mich.: Cistercian Publications), 49. Gertrude is remembered on November 16 in the Roman calendar.

37. *The Prayers of Catherine of Siena*, ed. Suzanne Noffke, O.P. (New York: Paulist Press, 1983), 78-79. Catherine's memorial falls on April 29 in the *Book of Common Prayer*, the Roman calendar, the *Lutheran Book of Worship*, and the Methodist calendar.

38. *Ancient Devotions to the Sacred Heart of Jesus by Carthusian Monks of the XIV-XVII Centuries* (Westminister, Md.: Newman Press, 1954), 196–197.

39. Margaret Mary is remembered on the Roman calendar on October 16.

40. The litany was written by St. John Eudes. Cf. *The Sacred Heart of Jesus*, trans. Dom Richard Flower (New York: P. J. Kenedy & Sons, 1946), 170-71. August 19 is Eudes's memorial in the Roman calendar.

41. Quoted in Ursula King, *Spirit of Fire: The Life and Vision of Teilhard de Chardin* (Maryknoll, N.Y.; Orbis Books, 1996), 204.

42. Sallie McFague, *The Body of God: An Ecological Theology* (Minneapolis, Minn.: Augsburg Fortress Press, 1993).

43. Text: Marty Haugen. © *1982 GIA* Publications Inc.

44. Ada María Isasi-Díaz and Yolanda Tarango, *Hispanic Women: Prophetic Voice in the Church.* (Minneapolis, Minn.: Augsburg Fortress Press, 1992), 16.

45. These images of Jesus, which portray his place in the history of culture, are taken from Jaroslav Pelikan's much admired book, *Jesus Through the Centuries: His Place in the History of Culture* (New York: HarperCollins, 1987).

46. Some accounts record the number as seventy.

47. Based on a prayer of Richard of Chichester, 1197-1253.

48. Benedict's memorial is July 11 on the Roman calendar and on the calendar for United Methodists, the *Book of Common Prayer,* and the *Lutheran Book of Worship.*

49. Scholastica is remembered on February 10 in the Roman rite.

50. Contemporary writers who have developed the ideas of spiritual disciplines are many. My favorites are Richard J. Foster, *Celebration of Discipline* (San Francisco: Harper and Row, 1988) and Marjorie Thompson, *Soul Feast* (Louisville, Ky.: Westminster, John Knox, 1995).

51. Bach and Handel are remembered on July 28 on the Methodist calendar. That calendar also includes Charles Wesley (March 29: "Hark the Herald Angels Sing," "Christ the Lord Is Risen Today," "Love Divine All Loves Excelling"); Fanny Jane Crosby (February 11: "Blessed Assurance"); Isaac Watts (November 25: "Joy to the World," "O God, Our Help in Ages Past"). The *Lutheran Book of Worship* also places Bach and Handel on July 28.

52. Text: Henry van Dyke, 1852-1933.

53. Esther de Waal, *Living with Contradictions: Reflections on the Rule of St. Benedict* (San Francisco: HarperSanFrancisco, 1989), 57-58.

54. Brother Lawrence, *The Practice of the Presence of God: Being Conversations and Letters of Nicholas Herman of Lorraine* (Westwood, N.J.: Fleming H. Revell Co., 1958), 49-50.

55. Text: Prayer attributed to Saint Francis.

56. Cf. Beverly Flanigan, *Forgiving the Unforgivable* (Old Tappan, N.J.: Macmillan, 1992).

57. Medieval Christians elaborated Martha's story as well as Mary Magdalene's. Martha was revered as a missionary possessed of great power who traveled as far as the south of France in her zeal to proclaim the good news. Today the churches celebrate her feast on July 29. She

is now held up as one who offers a full confession of Jesus as the Messiah. "Yes Lord," she said, "I believe that you are the Christ, the Son of God, the one who was to come into this world" (John 11:27, NJB; see also 20:31).

58. Jerimiah 8:22, Negro spiritual.

59. Ignatius of Loyola is remembered on the Roman calendar on July 31.

60. Flora Slosson Wuellner has written an excellent book on this subject, *Feed My Shepherds* (Nashville, Tenn.: Upper Room Books™, 1998).

61. Bunyan is remembered on August 31 on the Methodist and Lutheran calendars.

62. An accessible contemporary guide to Ignatian discernment can be found in Joan Mueller's *Faithful Listening: Discernment in Everyday Life* (St. Louis: Sheed and Ward, 1996).

63. Text 1 Corinthians 1:18: George W. Kitchen, 1827-1912 and Michael Newbolt 1874-1956, alt.

64. Parker J. Palmer, *The Promise of Paradox: A Celebration of Contradictions in the Christian Life* (Notre Dame, Ind.: Ava Maria Press 1980), 46.

65. The Triumph of the Cross or Feast of the Holy Cross falls on September 14.

66. From "The Victorious Cross," in Bless the Lord! (Notre Dame, Ind.: Ave Maria Press, 1974), 221.

67. *Vexilla Regis* prodent: Venantius Fortunatus, c. 530-609.

68. Cornelius is remembered in the Western church on September 16, Cyprian on the same day on the Roman calendar and on the 13 in the *Book of Common Prayer*.

69. Their memorials are located together on July 1 in the Eastern church and on September 26 or 27 in the Western churches.

70. The West commemorates him on September 19, the East on April 21.

71. The Korean martyrs are remembered on September 20 in the Roman church.

72. Memorials for Augustine, Ambrose, and Thomas Aquinas are, respectively, August 28, December 7, and January 28.

73. Negro spiritual.

74. The *Book of Common Prayer* and the Methodist calendar reserve September 29 for Michael and All Angels. In England Michael's day is

traditionally known as "Michaelmas Day." The Roman calendar memorializes Michael, Gabriel, and Raphael, Archangels on September 29 and the Guardian Angels on October 2. The Eastern church remembers Michael on November 8 and Gabriel on March 26.

75. Catherine of Siena, *The Dialogue*, trans. Suzanne Noffke, O.P. (New York: Paulist Press, 1980), 62.

76. Margaret Guenther, *Holy Listening: The Art of Spiritual Direction* (Cambridge, MA: Cowley Publications, 1992), 32, 38–39.

77. "The Rich Epicure and Poor Lazarus," from *The Gospel in Art by the Peasants of Solentiname*, ed. Philip and Sally Scharper (Maryknoll, N.Y.: Orbis Books, 1984), 30.

78. Text: Francis of Assisi; trans. William H. Draper, 1925.

79. Teresa is remembered on the Roman and the Methodist calendars in October. *The Lutheran Book of Worship* places her memorial on December 14.

80. Text: James Quinn, S. J., © 1969.

81. The prayers and order of evening prayer followed here are from the *Book of Common Worship* for the Presbyterian Church (U.S.A.) and the Cumerland Presbyterian Church. (Louisville, Ky.: Westminister, John Knox, 1993), 505 ff.

82. Phos Hilarion, Greek c. 200: text trans. William Storey, b. 1923 c. 1975 G.I.A. Publ, Inc.

83. Presbyterian *Book of Common Worship*, 61-62.

84. January 1 honors Mary as Mother of God; February 2 (the Presentation) includes a memorial of her Purification (as required by ancient Jewish law); February 11 celebrates one of the great modern Marian apparitions, at Lourdes; March 25 is the feast of the Annunciation (the angel Gabriel's announcement); May 31 is the Visitation (this is found in the *Book of Common Prayer* as well); on variable dates in May, the Roman church honors the heart of Mary, revered in tandem with her son's sacred heart; July 16 makes note of another apparition at Mount Carmel; Joachim and Anne, the man and woman who ancient accounts remember as her parents, are honored on the July 26; August 5 is the dedication of the Basilica of Saint Mary Major (Our Lady of the Snow); the Assumption of Mary (her bodily transport to heaven) falls on August 15 in the Roman calendar; August 22 honors her as queen; on September 8 her birth is celebrated; she is remembered as

the sorrowing mother on September 15; and as Our Lady of the Rosary October 7; November 21 finds her as a young girl being presented in temple; on December 8 Catholics celebrate her Immaculate Conception (the belief that at her conception in the womb of her mother, Mary was in some way freed from the effects of original sin).

85. The Joyful mysteries are the Annunciation, Visitation, Nativity, Presentation, and Finding of the Child Jesus in the Temple. The Sorrowful mysteries are the Agony in the Garden, the Scourging at the Pillar, the Crowning with Thorns, the Carrying of the Cross, the Crucifixion and Death of Jesus. The Glorious mysteries are the Resurrection, the Ascension of Christ, the Descent of the Spirit at Pentecost, the Assumption of Mary into Heaven, Mary's Coronation in Heaven as Queen.

86. Quoted in *Mother of God*, text by Lawrence Cunningham, photographs by Nicolas Sapieha (San Francisco: Harper and Row, 1982), 122.

87. Sandra Cronk, *Dark Night Journey: Inward Re-Patterning Toward a Life Centered in God* (Wallingford, Pa.: Pendle Hill, 1993), 59.

88. Text: Caroline V. Sandell-Berg, 1832-1903; tran. Ernst W. Olson, 1870-1958; trans. © Augsburg Fortress.

89. Hildegard of Bingen, Scivias, trans. Mother Columba Hart and Jane Bishop (New York: Paulist Press, 1990), 525, 527-28. Hildegard's day is celebrated on September 17 in many parts of Germany.

90. Text: *Nun danket alle Gott*: Martin Rinkart, 1586-1649; trans. Catherine Winkworth, 1827-1878, alt.

91. Text: William W. How, 1823-1897.

92. From the Lorica or "Breastplate," an ancient Celtic prayer attributed to Saint Patrick.

93. Negro spiritual.

94. William Blake, "The Little Black Boy," *Songs of Innocence*.

Pages 238-239 constitute an extension of the copyright page.

Scripture texts designated JB are taken from the Jerusalem Bible, published and copyright © 1966, 1967 and 1968 by Darton, Longman & Todd Ltd. and Doubleday & Co. Inc., and are used by permission of the publishers.

Scripture texts designated NJB are taken from the *New Jerusalem Bible*, published and copyright © 1985 by Darton, Longman & Todd Ltd. and Doubleday & Co. Inc., and are used by permission of the publishers.

Scripture texts or other quotations designated BCP are from the *Book of Common Prayer*, 1979 (according to the use of the Episcopal Church), published by the Church Hymnal Corporation, New York City.

Scripture texts designated AP are author's paraphrase.

Text to Psalm 63 adapted from the *Good News Bible*, second edition © 1992 American Bible Society. Used by permission.

Text of "Children of the Heavenly Father" © Board of Publication, Lutheran Church in America. Reprinted by permission of Augsburg Fortress.

Excerpts from *Catherine of Siena: The Dialogue*, trans. by Suzanne Noffke, O.P. Copyright © 1980 by The Missionary Society of St. Paul the Apostle in the State of New York, and from *Hildegard of Bingen: Scivias*, trans. by Mother Columba Hart and Jane Bishop, © 1990 by the Abbey of Regina Laudis: Benedictine Congregation Regina Laudis of the Strict Observance, Inc., are used by permission of Paulist Press Inc.

Psalm 141 on pages 187–188 is from *An Inclusive-Language Psalter of the Christian People*. Copyright © 1999 by The Order of St. Benedict, Inc. Published by The Liturgical Press, Collegeville, Minnesota. Used with permission.

Excerpt from *Gertrud the Great: Spiritual Exercises*, trans. by Gertrud Jaron Lewis and Jack Lewis. © 1989 Cistercian Publications, Kalamazoo, Michigan. Used by permission.

"The Rich Epicure and Poor Lazarus" from *The Gospel in Art by the Peasants of Solentiname*, ed. Philip and Sally Scharper. English language text copyright © 1984 by Orbis Books. Used by permission.

Excerpt from "Morning Has Broken" is from *The Children's Bells* by Eleanor Farjeon and is printed with permission of David Higham Associates, London.

Excerpt from "Day Is Done" by James Quinn, S.J. Published by Geoffrey Chapman, an imprint of Cassell & Co. Used by permission.

Excerpt from "Little Gidding" in *Four Quartets*, copyright © 1942 by T.S. Eliot and renewed 1970 by Esme Valerie Eliot. Reprinted by permission of Harcourt, Inc. and Faber & Faber, Ltd.

Excerpt from "Prayer of St. Francis." Dedicated to Mrs. Frances Tracy. Copyright © 1967 OCP Publications, 5536 NE Hassalo, Portland, OR 97213. All rights reserved. Used with permission.

Excerpt from "One Bread, One Body." Copyright © 1978 John B. Foley, SJ and New Dawn Music, 5536 NE Hassalo, Portland, OR 97213. All rights reserved. Used with permission.

Excerpt from "Here I Am, Lord." Copyright © 1981 Daniel L. Schutte and New Dawn Music, 5536 NE Hassalo, Portland, OR 97213. All rights reserved. Used with permission.

Excerpt from "Gather Us In" by Marty Haugen. Copyright © 1982 by GIA Publications, Inc. Chicago, IL. All rights reserved. Used with permission.

"O Radiant Light." Trans. copyright © William G. Storey. Used by permission.